Mortimer On Sports

Ray Scott's Going Places

By Jeff Mortimer

YPSILANTI — Ray Scott isn't going to be an assistant coach for long.

That might be a funny thing to say about somebody who's only had six assistant coach's job for a couple of weeks. But a person who talks to Earl Lloyd's new aide—camp with the Pistons quickly discovers that this is not a man who's going to settle into a nice, comfortable rut.

"I never set limits on myself...

Warriors' Foe Tonight

Pistons at Arena

By Dick Friendlich

Equipped with what should be a lot of firepower and a new coach in Earl Lloyd to lead them to victory in his first outing, the Detroit Pistons move into the Oakland Arena tonight. The Warriors...

EX-STAR ALSO TO SERVE AS SCOUT

Scott Named Piston Assistant Coach

By CURT SYLVESTER

"THAT DIDN'T make any difference in our decision," Coit explained. "What it boils down to..."

'OUR GOAL IS TO MAKE THE PLAYOFFS'

Pistons Find 'Mr. Enthusiasm'

thing pretty special. I guess everybody did. We'd win games any way we could—snatch 'em away in the closing seconds on a rebound. It was very remote...everybody felt it, from the bellhops to the management and the players...

AND NOW SCOTT is trying to implant same enthusiasm in an entire organization, all himself in the glorious place world of the Pistons.

"...there's such a lot of pessimism," said squirming at the thought of it all over the city. You can just feel it all.

"It's apathy," he continued. "The black man I can feel apathy even sunk into the ghetto. And that strong. It's a feeling of helplessness."

RAY SCOTT

69

Lanky Ray found a home for his all around play with the Bullets after controversial deal which brought him from Detroit in 1966-67. Averaged 11.8 points per game, was team's No. 2 rebounder.

CAREER NBA STATISTICS

THE BULLETS GOT RAY IN A THREE-TEAM TRADE IN 1966-67

Detroit Free Press

Rival coaches Ray Scott, left, of the Pistons and Tom Heinsohn of the Celtics exchange words before the start of Hall of Fame game Monday night at the Civic Center. The Celtics won, 119-117.

Scott: 'My Players Won It For Me'

Ray Scott had just won in his NBA coaching debut—but he wasn't about to take any credit for Detroit's victory over the Trail Blazers.

"Coaches don't win games," said the former University of Portland star. "I didn't win it for them. My players won it for me."

who played in 13 Pilots during

LITTLE SURPRISED BUT NOT SH

Pistons

THERE HAD been speculation that Lloyd would not even be back for the...season and that Ray Scott—the "basketball man"...and be running the team for the...Rolff quit early...

THE NBA IN BLACK AND WHITE

THE NBA IN BLACK AND WHITE

THE MEMOIR OF A TRAILBLAZING
NBA PLAYER AND COACH

RAY SCOTT
with CHARLEY ROSEN

and with an introduction by
EARL MONROE

SEVEN STORIES PRESS
NEW YORK • OAKLAND • LONDON

Seven Stories Press
140 Watts Street
New York, NY 10013
www.sevenstories.com

Library of Congress Cataloging-in-Publication Data in on file.

ISBN: 978-1-64421-198-4 (hardcover)
ISBN: 978-1-64421-199-1 (ebook)

College professors and high school and middle school teachers may order free examination copies of Seven Stories Press titles. Visit https://www.sevenstories.com/pg/resources-academics or email academics@sevenstories.com.

Printed in the USA.

9 8 7 6 5 4 3 2 1

To all of my wonderful grandchildren and great-grandchildren, and to all the other grandchildren and great-grandchildren in our country. Because they will hopefully have the power to transform this great experiment that's called the United States of America into "a more perfect union."

And to LeBron James, in appreciation for all he's done to enrich the lives of so many people in our community.

Let me remind you of that unfulfilled promise, the one

right there in the Declaration of Independence: "All

men are created equal." I've been waiting my whole

life for America to live up to that.

—Bill Russell

CONTENTS

INTRODUCTION by Earl Monroe xi

ACKNOWLEDGMENTS xv

PROLOGUE 3

PART ONE

CHAPTER ONE: My Beginnings 9

CHAPTER TWO: Learning the *Hamotzi*,
Playing in the Baker, and UP. 17

CHAPTER THREE: Not Such a Big Man on Campus,
Then Far East of the NBA. 31

CHAPTER FOUR: Anointed by the Dipper 39

CHAPTER FIVE: A Stranger in Paradise 49

CHAPTER SIX: Black Man Out. 63

CHAPTER SEVEN: In These Changing Times 67

PART TWO

CHAPTER EIGHT: Looking Back 73

CHAPTER NINE: Civil Rights and Un-Civil Wrongs 79

CHAPTER TEN: The Brothers Change the Games
and Their Names 93
CHAPTER ELEVEN: Forever Didn't Last Long 103

PART THREE

CHAPTER TWELVE: That's What I Like About
the South. 117
CHAPTER THIRTEEN: Detroit Redux with a Few
Major Surprises. 123
CHAPTER FOURTEEN: "Bennie and the Jets". 129
CHAPTER FIFTEEN: The Not-So-Fortunate Fall 137
CHAPTER SIXTEEN: How Bob Ferry Showed Me
the Way to Build a Championship Team. 145
CHAPTER SEVENTEEN: The Beginning of the End,
and the Blood on My Back 147

PART FOUR

CHAPTER EIGHTEEN: Abracadabra, and the
NBA Flies High 157
CHAPTER NINETEEN: Same Game, New Rules 167
CHAPTER TWENTY: Against the Wind. 185
CHAPTER TWENTY-ONE: The NBA Then and Now 203
CHAPTER TWENTY-TWO: Welcome to My America 221

INDEX. 231
ABOUT THE AUTHORS 240

INTRODUCTION

by Earl Monroe

I rarely make public comments about anything people I know have written or said, but I'm happy to make an exception here.

Ray and I were both born and raised in the same South Philly neighborhood, six years apart. I never got the chance to meet or see Ray play because I didn't get interested in basketball until I was fourteen, when the junior high school coach saw this skinny 6'3" kid walking down the hall and asked if I played basketball. For me it was a life-changing moment.

I was a junior at John Bartram High School when I first saw Ray play. He had just finished his rookie year with the Detroit Pistons, and had come back to Philly to play in the Baker League. He often came over to the neighborhood basketball courts to work out and play with some of his friends. Even though Ray had the exalted stature, in my eyes, of being an NBA player, he treated me and all the other young players with total respect, shaking hands and acknowledging us. He probably didn't even notice I was there, as we young guys used to sit around the edge of the court hoping to get picked to play the winners in the next game. We never got picked. Later, when I was playing at Winston-Salem, I started to play in the legendary Philadelphia–New York Games in the summer. He played in the pro game, and I played in the college game. That's when I joined Ray in the traditional brotherhood of "Philadelphia basketball players."

Eventually Ray and I were teammates with the Baltimore Bullets from 1967 to 1970, and our friendship deepened. Working and traveling with the team, we wound up spending a lot of time together, both on and off the court, going to dinner, movies, and shows or just hanging out at the clubs on Baltimore Street, like the Casino, where some of the greats in R&B and jazz played every night. Artists like Stevie Wonder, Gladys Knight & the Pips, the Four Tops, the Temptations, Les McCann, and many more made their way through Baltimore. It was the gateway between the North and the South, depending on which way you were traveling.

Ray and I talked about everything at that time—from basketball strategy to our observations of local, national, and NBA politics. We even had the chance to travel to Japan together, along with Bob Ferry for the State Department, where we visited the tragic burn wards of our soldiers who had been injured and maimed during the Vietnam War.

I always appreciated Ray's talent and his will to win. Boy, with the way he handled the ball and his shooting range, he really would have loved to play in *this* edition of the NBA. But even more than that, I simply enjoyed him as a good-hearted, perceptive person with a terrific head on his shoulders when it came to both the game of basketball and the dynamics of our American culture. Over the entire span of the sixty years I've known him, he's always remained true to himself, whether as a professional athlete, an NBA or college coach, or when he was selling insurance.

Given our common background, the racial situation was always central to our discussions, both the prejudice that we each faced and the pervasive bias that still confronts our people. Our views were, and still are, identical in this regard. We're both aware that, despite some significant missteps, race relations have evolved and improved over the years of the NBA's existence, and we're looking forward to seeing that evolution influence our country as a whole. After all, as a people, we've been here for four hundred years, well before America even became a country. We've fought for this country and have made significant contributions to this country, and it's shameful that we still need to have laws passed to enable us to vote. Studying American history is often like studying partial truths. All the stories are centered around white existence and heroic deeds and there's very little about the Black experience and how we've endured the brutality and oppressions—and yet we're still here!

Ray Scott has given us all a good read with his book, a thoughtful and heartful narrative of some of what he's seen and experienced. Myself, I've learned a lot that I didn't know about Ray, his family, and how he has navigated his way through life. The book is inspiring and, to me, enlightening.

He takes the reader inside the locker room to reveal how players feel about each other, about their coaches, about the media, and about management. Along the way, Ray also gives us personal, in-depth scouting reports of Wilt Chamberlain, Bill Russell, Magic Johnson, Larry Bird, Willis Reed, and many more. Readers will find eye-opening discussions about how much individual and team rivalries greatly enhanced the popularity of the league and made it an avenue for the riches present-day athletes enjoy.

Ray Scott may be a modest person, but he's had a big life. He's known other great athletes, such as Muhammad Ali and Joe Frazier, and gives us a ringside seat. Ray was part of the action, as a team rep, when the owners certified the NBA players union in 1964. He was also right there in 1970, when the historic Oscar Robertson suit was filed. It wasn't entirely settled until 1976, but as a result and ever since then, players have had the right to declare free agency.

Throughout the book, Ray dishes out some inside information, but never deviates from his honorable purpose—which is not to shock but to make his readers *think* about NBA basketball and the progress the league has made in the sensitive issue of race in America.

Ray is neither an NBA apologist nor an NBA critic. He just tells it like he saw it, which is exactly the way it was and is.

Earl Monroe
New York City

ACKNOWLEDGMENTS

I'd like to thank the team:

DAN SIMON, for believing in my story.

RUTH WEINER, for her wonderful guidance.

My writing partner, CHAZZ, who created this opportunity to embark on our journey with Seven Stories Press.

DAIA GERSON, whose editing simply thrilled me when I saw how it took the book to another level.

THE NBA IN BLACK AND WHITE

PROLOGUE

My name is John Raymond Scott, but I'm better known as Ray. I was born on July 12, 1938, at the Frederick Douglass Memorial Hospital, in a Black neighborhood in South Philadelphia.

I have been blessed to have played in the National Basketball Association for nine years (1961–70) and in the American Basketball Association (ABA) for two years (1970–72), and to have coached the Detroit Pistons from 1972 to 1976. At the end of the 1973–74 regular season I was named the NBA's Coach of the Year, the first African American to be so honored. Then, when standing at midcourt at halftime of a subsequent playoff game against the Chicago Bulls in Cobo Hall, receiving the trophy, I was even more amazed when the SRO crowd of eleven thousand hometown fans got to their feet to cheer me wildly.

Several questions are basic to my story: How did I, a kid from a low-rent, third-floor walk-up apartment in South Philly who started playing basketball when I was ten, go where I've been and get to where I am? How and why did I manage to survive the usual racial obstacles that hindered and often destroyed the careers and lives of so many Black men, including basketball players who I believe were more talented than I ever was? Some of these questions are relatively easy for me to answer. Some I'm still trying to figure out.

Like everyone else I knew, I'd grown up hearing about the routine racial discrimination adults in my family and in my neighborhood were forced to endure. But my personal awakening came as a twelve-year-old, when my uncle took my brother and me on a trip to Washington, DC. I saw the care he had to take to only drive along "safe" highways and only stop at "safe" gas stations. We were driving deeper into the South, after all, and were no longer in friendly Philadelphia. And now, in our nation's capital, I was disturbed to see "Colored Only" water fountains.

Four years later, when I was sixteen and the horrible details of fourteen-year-old Emmett Till's murder became public, I was stunned to realize that this could happen to me, too, and to any one of my friends. Like too many other children of color, I might have succumbed to the stress of this overwhelming reality of African American life if it had not been for the loving presence of a father (actually, my stepfather).

By the time I was twenty-two and a rookie in the NBA, I had more money than ever in my pocket. I already knew that having a healthy bankroll was the key to some measure of validation in this culture. Now I was traveling the country and, with an expanded view, could sense a dawning recognition of widespread racial inequality. I was waking up and so was the rest of American society.

It was the early sixties, and JFK promised to include Black people in the mainstream of America's new dream. The US Supreme Court outlawed blatant racial segregation. Voting rolls were expanded in Black communities. Previously all-white colleges were beginning to recruit Black athletes in ever-increasing numbers. Positive things were happening all over the map.

Both my life and my times have led me to several conclusions. Here are a few of them, with many more to come:

That there are still many struggles ahead, both individually and collectively, but positive changes *are* happening. So we must all be persistent in doing our part to make this a better world.

That, as an African American, and despite my successes, I still believe that if my people have not achieved equality, then I have not achieved equality.

That even though Black people want to evolve socially, politically, and legally, there are no rules to guide us in this collective endeavor.

That each of us has to find our own way.

My purpose, then, in writing this book is to explore, and hopefully to encourage a better understanding of, a certain portion of the history of "We the people" as I have experienced it. My ultimate aim is not to shock but to encourage readers to think.

What follows is my best attempt to explain how I've succeeded, also how I've failed, and how my path might encourage readers to open-mindedly face their own journey.

Basketball in Catskills Rises to Ne

Tall Athletes Work Out on Court After Work on Dishes

By WILLIAM R. CONKLIN
Special to The New York Times.

MONTICELLO, N. Y., Aug. 10
—Those who get closest to the ps of the Catskill Mountains re without climbing are eight itud
h a
mul
ro
he
ics
al

Ray Sc...s.. To Join Pisto

By MIKE LITTWIN
the detroit sports writer

Ray Scott, among the most popular players ever to wear a Virginia Squire uniform, will leave the organization soon to accept a position with the Detroit Pistons of the National Basketball Association.

A source close to Scott told the Times-Herald today that the 35-year veteran will serve the Pistons as an assistant coach and super scout beginning Sept. 1.

Scott, who retired at the end of last season to join the front office in the role of sales representative, has officially tendered his resignation to co-owner Earl Foreman.

Given coach Earl Lloyd the Scott the top job last Felix, but the native Philadel- decided to give Fore- offer a chance. upon accepting then that poor noted ly reject, his adjust- de park.

dly it was not his

University of Fort-as returns to the arly days in pro- betball. After two Eastern League, forward broke bus. star for Det. and then the

not available often said to return to was quite a boxing

of what take " inter.

referred e human b sins of the past.

dependable player two sea- sons ago when he came to Virginia after jumping from the NBA. Though the second string scorer, he far out- played Jim Eakins in the pivot.

And when the going was rough, Scott was there.

last year he was used quite sparingly by Bianchi until the season's end and when he once again starred.

Scott was quite openly dis- gusted with the manner in which he was played. And it no doubt contributed to his re- tirement.

Scott had his most produc- tive years in the NBA with the Pistons.

This marks the second Squire who has left the orga- nization to become an assis- tant coach. Doug Moe, whose retirement was forced upon him last year by a set of bad

knots, is an old-Squire teams Brown with the Co- gars.

With the certain of Scott, that leaves ership void on the who now boast one youngest teams in the

SQUIRES
22

Pressure

Scott expects top Pistons to produc

BY BILL HALEY
News Sports Writer

Shortly after Ray Scott, opened his

227

A native of played high Chamberlai 11,000 NBA big men

CHAPTER ONE

MY BEGINNINGS

I was named after my maternal grandfather, John Raymond Mackey, a steel worker living in Youngstown, Ohio, who would frequently come to visit us in Philly. He was handsome, austere, intelligent, well-read, and he encouraged my early interest in books. As I grew, we stayed connected, and years later, when he died in 1963, my mom and I attended his funeral in Youngstown.

My biological father, John Samuel Howard, simply vanished when I was one year old. My mother remarried three years later. My stepfather, Sylvester Bernard Scott, gave me love, security, a new last name and, most importantly, he gave me a family. All the things that the four-year-old me really needed. I was heartbroken at age eight when he passed.

There's an enormous body of literature that says African American boys raised by single mothers have difficult lives ahead of them. Indeed, 72 percent of "Negro" males in America are raised by single mothers—as opposed to 25.8 percent of the total population. These youngsters are at a higher risk of engaging in drug and alcohol abuse, of being less cooperative with authority figures, of having damaging emotional problems, and of possessing a weaker sense of right and wrong.

Growing up as poor as we were might have been another considerable handicap, but I didn't realize we were poor, because everybody that I knew was in the same situation. I escaped all of these potential problems through the loving attentions of my mother, who taught her children to always look for the value and humanity in everybody we encounter.

And I also survived these obstacles through my involvement in basketball.

I began my on-court future at the Western Community House when I was eight. The tiny basketball court on the second floor attracted most of my attention, and there were many days when I practiced there on my own. That's where I played my first Biddy League game two years later. There I was, a squeaky-voiced kid so excited that I didn't know what to do. I probably didn't do anything extraordinary during my Biddy League days, because I don't remember any of the games.

But I do remember being excited when I played in my first road game. This was at the Phillis Wheatley Recreation Center, located in a residential neighborhood in North Philly. I remember playing there because Phillis Wheatley (1753–84) had been enslaved in Boston but had developed into one of the most popular poets in the late eighteenth century. She was especially revered in Philadelphia, so I knew she was a hero.

My solo practice sessions started to pay off when I was eleven. By the time I was fourteen and in the ninth grade, I was 6'3" and had a fantasy that I could be a good player.

I had another early epiphany when I was twelve and my Uncle Reese drove me and my younger brother, Marvin, on a long-promised trip to Washington, DC. On our way there, we drove through Delaware and Maryland, with Uncle Reese strictly following the traveling guide in *The Negro Motorist Green Book* that had been written by Victor Hugo Green in 1936 and updated in subsequent editions. There were no superhighways, and a scarcity of welcoming gas stations and restaurants on our route, so the listing of the safest/quickest roads was Uncle Reese's only game plan. But I was so excited that I paid no attention to our routes and stops.

I had heard about the Jim Crow laws when people discussed them back in Philly—in living rooms, drugstores, restaurants, and churches. However, it was in our nation's capital that I first saw "White" and "Colored" water fountains. The first time we boarded a trolley, I immediately went to the front of the car like I always did back home, but I was sternly told that I had to move to the back. Likewise, when we went to see a movie, I tried to sit in my usual front-row seat, until I was grabbed by the arm and told I had to sit in the balcony—another rude and unexpected slap in the face for twelve-year-old me.

We stayed for a week at a small townhouse that Uncle Reese owned in a segregated neighborhood. Back in Philly, we used to picnic at Fairmount Park, which was integrated. So the total absence of any white people in this DC neighborhood was another shock.

However, I did have an unexpected positive experience there. One of the neighborhood kids took me to a playground, saying, "You gotta see Rabbit play."

"Rabbit" turned out to be sixteen years old, maybe 6′5″, about 235 pounds, and was simply unstoppable. With his drives, dunks, jumpers, and rebounds, he never lost a game. He wasn't a step above the other players, he was a full staircase above them.

And Rabbit's real name was Elgin Baylor.

Elgin and I were destined to meet again many times both on and off the court.

Even so, the racial bias I had experienced in DC dominated my mind and my mood. So, on the drive back to Philly, I now paid more attention to the routes and the stops Uncle Reese made. When we were hungry we had to go to the back door of a restaurant to order our food, then eat in the car. When we had to relieve ourselves, we had to pee in the bushes. Even so, Uncle Reese always told us to hurry up because any cop that happened by could arrest us for indecent exposure.

I realized that racism was the rule in American culture. It was true then, and it still holds true today.

The next significant step up was a two-year stint at South Catholic High School, where I played on the frosh and then the JV teams. I had grown to 6'6", and despite my rail-thin body, I averaged 25 points for the JV. They tried to keep me happy by promising that in my junior and senior years I'd be an important varsity player, but I was never promoted to the varsity.

Meanwhile, it was the summer after my freshman year that I started playing at least three times a week in neighborhood games with some terrific Philly guys: Woody Sauldsberry, "Bozo" Walker, "Puny" Bill Murray, Hal Lear, Guy Rodgers, Wayne Hightower, and John Chaney. Players from other neighborhoods would come to our playground, and we'd make the rounds of theirs. That was my first introduction to big-time basketball. I didn't embarrass myself too often, and I sure did learn a lot.

Unfortunately, South Catholic was in a tough Italian neighborhood, and I was beaten up several times for the crime of being Black. The principal claimed that I had started the fights because *I* was a bully! So, after my sophomore year I transferred to a public school. I could handle, shoot, and rebound, so for the next two seasons at West Philadelphia High School I was named to All-City teams.

Wilt Chamberlain was a senior at Overbrook High School when I was a junior. We lost only three games that season, all of them to Wilt and company. With Wilt off to Kansas, we won the Public League championship, beating Northeast High School, whose star player was Herb Adderley. My efforts were ably abetted by a pair of very talented teammates—Carl Lacy and Hubie White.

Yet, even as a high-schooler, I echoed certain concerns of the adults in my community. By reading *Jet*, *EBONY*, and the local Black newspapers, as well as listening to talk around my neighborhood, I learned about the fate that befell many Black soldiers in Europe during World War II. A disproportionate number of executions for capital crimes in Europe during the war were doled out to Black soldiers, and among the atrocities suffered by those who weren't executed were various forms of mutilation.

Moreover, some Black veterans who survived the war and returned home were subjected to the same kind of overt discrimination that they had endured before they risked their lives for their country.

These incidents angered just about every African American I encountered.

So, yes, my brothers and sisters helped win the war "over there," but were still on the losing end of the war here.

It should be noted that President Eisenhower's highway construction program in the early and mid-1950s deserves major credit for enabling African American schoolyard/playground players to have easier access to competitive pickup games in other neighborhoods and even other cities. This included more opportunities to play in white neighborhoods. This was a development that greatly accelerated my own on-court growth.

Moreover, the creation of America's "autobahn"—its system of highways—was a boon to those African Americans who sought to drive their cars to visit friends and relatives in the South. No longer did they have to depend on *The Green Book* to inform them which were the safe roads to take on these trips and which were the dangerous ones. No more fearful trips through towns hostile to Blacks, especially those in cars with Northern license plates. Instead, they could now cruise at high speed in relative safety along the new superhighways.

When I was in high school, four of Philly's Big 5 colleges and universities (Saint Joseph's, Villanova, La Salle, and Penn) fielded all-white basketball teams. Meanwhile, a trio of Black players— Guy Rodgers, Hal "King" Lear, and Jay Norman—starred for Temple. Accordingly, most of the Blacks in Philadelphia never rooted for the four teams that didn't recruit African Americans. And I've always believed that the Big 5 made a huge mistake by letting Wilt get out of town. They should have pooled their resources to do whatever had to be done to keep him in Philly.

Ever since Jackie Robinson integrated baseball in 1947, Black people wanted to see more African Americans participate in all sports. So, whenever we could scrape together enough money for tickets, my buddies and I would go to the Palestra to watch as many Temple games as possible. We were also eager to see visiting teams that likewise featured Black players facing any of the Big 5: Seton Hall with Dick Gaines and Walter Dukes. St. Francis (NY) with Vernon Stokes and Al Inniss. St. Francis

(PA) with the incredible Maurice Stokes. Manhattan with Junius Kellogg. And, of course, Duquesne with Sihugo Green and the Ricketts brothers. Occasionally we would even drive up to New York to see Providence's Lenny Wilkens play at Madison Square Garden.

Just to watch these guys play at such a high level in front of huge crowds was inspirational.

CHAPTER TWO

LEARNING THE *HAMOTZI*, PLAYING IN THE BAKER, AND UP

After my success at West Philly High School, I was recruited by several colleges. However, since I was aware of the racism that was rampant in so many schools and in so many parts of the country, I did a tremendous amount of research to discover which colleges already had Black players and which colleges had road games scheduled in places that were hostile to "Negroes." Here's what I found:

Willie Naulls and Walter Torrance were at UCLA.

Branch McCracken was always eager to recruit African Americans, so his team at Indiana had Walt Bellamy, Hallie Bryant, and Charley Brown. Later, Brown transferred to Seattle.

Elgin Baylor, of course, was at Seattle.

Michigan State had "Jumpin'" Johnny Green and Horace Walker.

San Francisco had Bill Russell and K.C. Jones.

The University of the Pacific had LeRoy Wright.

Clarence "Big House" Gaines paid a visit to my home and encouraged me to accept a scholarship to Winston-Salem. He said that if I was interested, I should meet him at a certain corner with my bags packed at a certain time the next day. But I was still making up my mind, so I never showed up.

I was interested in two other schools that contacted me, what at the time was known as Maryland State and Morgan State. Years later, these schools would be among the group collectively known as Historically Black Colleges and Universities, or HBCUs. But I remained undecided because I was still being recruited by other schools.

Illinois sent an assistant coach to my home, and the University of Oklahoma sent Benjamin Hooks, the vice president of the NAACP in Norman, Oklahoma. The latter's pitch was that I would be the first African American to play for the school. But both Urbana-Champaign and Norman were too far from Philly for me to go there. So I never gave a definitive answer to any of the schools that wanted me.

Except, that is, for NYU.

An ex-Knick, Ray Lumpp, was the dynamic assistant coach at NYU, and before he reached out to me, he had already signed up four African American high school players from New York City— Tom "Satch" Sanders, Al Barden, Russ Cunningham, and Cal Ramsey. Because of the racial quotas then in effect, I figured that at most only three of us would start, and since I'd be the only out-of-towner, I'd wind up on the bench. So I turned Lumpp down.

I had graduated from high school in January, but I was still unsure of which college scholarship I would accept. Then a friend called to say he could get me a scholarship at a junior college in New York City, where I could play for the rest of their season. It sounded like the perfect gig.

New York City Tech Junior College was situated in Downtown Brooklyn at 300 Jay Street. In addition to free tuition I was granted $15 every two weeks for "laundry money." And I hooped.

For what I expected to be the long haul, I moved in with Bernie Tiebout, a teammate. Except for an occasional dinner invitation, we didn't eat out much and not very well in. But the basketball competition was terrific. And I'm still in contact with Bernie.

Being a member of a basketball team at any level is a unique and total bonding experience that can last a lifetime. Baseball teams have dozens of players and different coaches for the pitchers, catchers, infielders, and so on. And football teams have so many players that some of them don't even know each other. But basketball teams have, at the most, maybe ten to twelve players, so the connection between teammates is much tighter.

Jerry Anderson was the coach and he had a structured game plan that perfectly suited me. I was soon established as the team's high scorer, and was the MVP in 1958 when we won the New York State Junior College Tournament.

I can't remember the courses that I took at City Tech, but I do recall dropping out of school as soon as the tournament was over. And I started a job search, applying to a bank, a department store, and a drug company, with no takers.

I was rescued, and not for the last time, by Haskell Cohen.

I had first connected with Haskell when I was sixteen and he was in charge of compiling a list of the country's best high school players for *Parade* magazine. Whenever he was in Philly, Haskell would take me to watch NBA games at Convention Hall, and try to convince me to go to either Duquesne and be coached by Donald "Dudey" Moore or play under John "Honey" Russell at Seton Hall.

Haskell was really a brilliant guy and had previously been the publicist for the Basketball Association of America (BAA) and then the post-merger NBA. Through the years, Haskell had encouraged NBA teams to draft African American players. He was strictly a New York guy and was instrumental in the Knicks trading for Ray Felix (1954) and then drafting Walter Dukes (1955). He knew everybody and everything that had to do with the NBA.

He was also the publicist for Kutsher's Country Club so he got in touch with me and arranged for me to spend a summer there working as a bellhop. Besides earning some money, the main attraction was the chance to play against college All-Americans from all over the country whom Haskell had arranged to work there as waiters, bellhops, and lifeguards.

There were several similar hotels in the Catskill Mountains area known as the Borscht Belt—Grossinger's, the Nevele, Brown's, the Granit, the Pines—that catered to Jewish customers, mostly from New York City and New Jersey. These places were built in the 1930s, when Jews were not allowed entrance into the other upstate hotels. In addition to Kutsher's, all the other hotels in the same circuit had highly competitive basketball teams, likewise featuring high school and collegiate standouts who also had service jobs.

When I worked there, all of the waiters and busboys at Kutsher's were white, while three of the ten bellhops were Black. One of my coworkers and new teammates was Al Butler from Niagara, who went on to have a productive four-year NBA run with Boston, New York, and Baltimore.

Besides the games and scrimmages we played, the highlight of that summer of 1958 was a pro All-Star game organized by Haskell and Red Auerbach. In addition to being the coach of the Boston Celtics, Auerbach was also on the payroll at Kutsher's as the resort's athletic director. The game was played on a Tuesday night in August, and Red brought several members of his Boston Celtics to play against other NBA players. Red's team featured Bob Cousy, Bill Sharman, and Tom Heinsohn.

(Bill Russell was there but had a sprained ankle and didn't play.) Their opponents included Paul Arizin, Carl Braun, Richie Guerin, Walt Bellamy, and Al Bianchi. Mendy Rudolph was the referee, one of the sharpest dressers I've ever seen. His animated foul calls were also part of the show. Even though the game was on a hard outdoor court, everybody played smart, hustling basketball. Some of the players would bring their families and stay for several days on the cuff.

The idea was to provide glamorous entertainment for Kutsher's guests. The game also attracted many of the guests from the other Catskills hotels, eager to witness NBA stars in the flesh. There was no admission charge, but the outsiders would certainly arrive early for drinks and dinner.

In the summers after Wilt Chamberlain's freshman and sophomore years at Kansas, he also worked as a bellhop at Kutsher's. Milt Kutsher loved him and, through the years, Wilt considered him to be a second father. But Milt's wife, Helen, complained when Milt originally said they'd have to build a bigger bed to accommodate Wilt. "Why not hire a shorter bellhop?" she asked.

"Because Wilt is going to be special."

Helen soon agreed, and according to her son, Mark, Wilt said, "Most people are happy with one set of parents. I've been blessed to have two."

There were several noteworthy college football players also working service jobs when Wilt first appeared on the scene, and they constantly bragged about how strong they were. Much stronger than this twenty-year-old kid. But when they challenged him to a weight-lifting contest, it became clear that he was way out of their league. Subsequently, a few of the football players hated Wilt.

Another reason they were probably not fond of him was because Wilt was the highest-earning bellhop in the history of the Borscht Belt. Even then, Wilt was special enough to use his enormous, record-setting tips to buy an expensive, personally fitted sports car when he left Kansas after his junior year.

Auerbach loved playing tennis, golf, as well as playing pinochle for cash. So, under his auspices, Red and many of the guests convened a Saturday-night pinochle game. I knew the reason why I was chosen to service their pinochle—getting ice, drinks, getting food, getting change for large bills. That's because Haskell and Red were buddies and both of them were prompting me to go to either Seton Hall or Duquesne. For every game I worked, I'd get really good tips—from $100 to $150.

The guests usually checked in on Friday nights and the men left Sunday to start their jobs back in the city on Monday. Often, wives and children stayed through the week, and the place livened up. But the ladies got religion on Friday. And everybody came dressed up in really fancy clothes for Friday dinner and the entertainment that followed!

The food was really incredible. Three separate and bountiful kosher meals! (Although there was one course I never liked, and that was the matzoh ball soup.) Even now, I can still remember the *Hamotzi* prayer that was chanted by everybody before each meal.

Baruch atah Adonai Eloheinu Melech ha'olam, hamotzi lechem min ha'aretz.

Blessed art Thou oh Lord our God, King of the universe who bringeth forth bread from the Earth.

Of course there were guests who ignored us brothers, some who treated us as anonymous servants, but most guests were warm and friendly. It was a snapshot of society in general.

Milt Kutsher's philosophy was very clear: "Everybody is on the same plane and must be treated with respect."

Really, if there had been any hint of expressed racism, Red never would have brought his players there.

I was also blown away by the entertainment. On weekends, Kutsher's headliner was Henny Youngman. And Henny always cracked me up.

"Take my wife.... Please."

"A nearsighted guy walks in to rob a bank. 'Hands up,' he says. 'Are they up?'"

Rodney Dangerfield was another comic who made me laugh to beat the band.

When we had nights free, we'd drive over to the other clubs to see their stage shows: Maybe Jerry Lewis, Steve and Eydie, Joey Adams, "Peg Leg" Bates, Buddy Hackett, Danny Kaye, Red Buttons, or Shelley Berman. Or we'd drive into Monticello to eat pizza and drink beer.

My fellow workers spent most of their off-hours relaxing and hanging out in the Deli and the staff bar. So did I, but I also spent a lot of my free time on the basketball court. Working on my game. Getting more rhythm in my shots.

We were not allowed in the pool where the famous Simon Sez games were conducted. But we were allowed to join the poolside dancing lessons. That's where I learned to cha-cha-cha, to mambo, and to do the meringue.

Of course the music in all the hotels was terrific: Machito and his band. Eddie Palmieri. Tito Puente. Tito Rodríguez. Pete Terrace. Also Cal Tjader. It was a musical education for me.

There was another All-Star game the following summer, but admission was charged because this one had a very different purpose. It was promoted and organized by Jack Twyman to raise money for the care of Maurice Stokes, a former teammate of his. Stokes had been a truly great NBA player with the Rochester/Cincinnati Royals (1955–58) who had been a three-time All-Star, Rookie of the Year, and league-leading rebounder. Tragically, he suffered a fall during a game that resulted in his eventually being diagnosed as having traumatic encephalopathy, a brain disease that damaged his motor control. This game eventually became the annual Maurice Stokes Game in which dozens of NBA stars paid their own expenses to participate.

I would be invited back to Kutsher's after the 1973–74 NBA season to coach one of the teams in a Stokes Game organized by Red Auerbach, who was also my opposing coach. Of course, Red stacked his team around the low-post play of Walt Bellamy. My guys included George McGinnis, Lloyd B. Free, and Wilt, who seemed to grab every rebound. And we won.

This was also Wilt's last timed and officiated game against other pros.

On this occasion I was treated like royalty and given my own luxurious room. This welcome would be extended to me every time I returned to Kutsher's from then on—except for one day when, for some reason, there were no such rooms available.

I was saved by Artie Heyman, an All-American from Duke. He was headed back to New York right after playing in the Stokes Game, so he gave me the key to his room. When I got there, the bathroom was ankle deep in water. That knucklehead hadn't closed the shower curtain when he showered.

Artie had been drafted by the Knicks and, before he left, he told me that he was going to take Richie Guerin's job in the backcourt. It was all I could do not to laugh in Artie's face. Guerin was in his prime, routinely averaging more than 20 points per game, once (1961–62) recording 29.5. Also, Richie was a native New Yorker out of Iona College in New Rochelle, and an ex-Marine. There was no way that Richie wouldn't destroy Artie.

Turned out Artie had a pretty good rookie season in New York (15.6 points), until his lack of speed, leaden jump shot, and defensive deficiency caught up with him. After getting booted from the Knicks, and only short stays in Cincinnati and Philadelphia, Artie also wore out his welcome, after two years, in the American Basketball Association.

And Richie kept pumping in the points.

I'm always amazed when players with obvious shortcomings in their games think that they're way, way better than they really are.

Anyway, putting Artie Heyman aside, I really developed a good feeling for my Jewish brothers and sisters. I had known many of them back in South Philly, where they owned several stores—butchers, groceries, and the like—and lived in apartments above them. So my connection with the guests at Kutsher's was more of a continuation than a revelation. I never felt left out and always had fun there. Over the course of that special summer, I did a lot of growing up. Learning to dance, seeing star performers in person whom I'd previously only seen on TV, and just experiencing a new culture expanded my life.

When I got back to Philly, I got a call from Al Negratti, the coach from the University of Portland (UP). He said that he had heard about me, and since he was visiting some relatives in New Jersey, he wondered if he could come to Philly and speak to me and my mother. Since I still hadn't picked a school, I readily agreed. He said he would show up that same evening, and he did.

When he arrived, Negratti simply took over the living room like he was Sammy Davis Jr. He informed me that Andy Johnson had starred at UP and went on to play for the Globe-trotters and the Philadelphia Warriors. Also, that if I accepted Negratti's offer, I'd have Jim Armstrong and Wally Panel as my teammates, two African Americans from Chicago who were called "The Whirlwind Twins." By then, I was ready to sign whatever he put in front of me.

Since my mom was a devout Catholic, when Negratti said that the college had close ties with Notre Dame, the best Catholic school in the country, she, too, was sold. And that was that.

I didn't even care that Portland was farther away from Philly than Norman was. But since I had never been in an airplane and was afraid to fly, Negratti agreed to accompany me on a three-day train ride to UP. While onboard "The City of Roses," I slept in a first-class berth and ate as much first-class food as I wanted. All the while, Negratti doubled down on the promises he had already made—I'd have a full room-board-and-books scholarship and I would immediately be a starter.

I was agreeable to everything Negratti said, except when he pointed to my mustache and said this: "How about you get rid of that cookie duster?"

I refused, but did accede to his suggestion once I got settled on campus.

It turned out that the 6'3" Negratti had been a key player at Seton Hall when the team went 71–7 from 1939 to 1943. Then, after serving in the military, he played in eleven games for the Washington Capitols in the 1946–47 season before the Basketball Association of America became the NBA. He also turned out to be a terrific coach, a great guy whose word was his bond.

Our first game of the season was at the University of Seattle, where Elgin Baylor would be starting his senior season (when he would average 32.5 points and 19.8 rebounds). So the day before the game, Jim Armstrong and I went over to Seattle's campus in hopes of hooking up with Elgin. And, lo and behold, there he was walking down a path and headed toward us.

After we introduced ourselves, Elgin said, "I'm going to the movies. You guys want to come?"

Yes!

He drove us there, we paid for our own tickets, and I'll never forget the movies that we saw:

Hemingway's *A Farewell to Arms* starring Rock Hudson and Jennifer Jones—one of the best movies I've ever seen. I was so impressed that I eventually bought and read every book Hemingway ever wrote.

The second feature was *Outlaw's Son*. Before this one started, Elgin said, "It has to be a B-movie because it stars Dane Clark and it's in black and white."

Elgin wasn't so friendly the next night in the season opener for both schools. I scored 28, but Elgin led his team to the win in a relatively close game by scoring 64!

I still hadn't seen him lose.

Here's another epiphany: The scene was a game in Portland between two barnstorming teams made up of outstanding NBA players: Neil Johnson, Cliff Hagan, and George Yardley—the original "Bird" who was the first NBA player to score 2,000 points in a season.

We sat in the first row and I was dazzled by the size and the skills of these guys. That's when Negratti told me words that I'll never forget: "If you work hard, Ray, and do what I think you can do, then you can be an NBA player."

I had always been a hard worker, but the prospect that Negratti raised made me work even harder. He was one of the wonderful people who did much to shape my life.

Later on, when Negratti's prediction came to pass, I spent a few summers visiting various friends in New York. That's when I discovered the games at Rucker Park up in Harlem. I'd guess that I played maybe two games every year on that legendary ballcourt. As a bona fide NBA player, I enjoyed competing against such luminaries as Herman "Helicopter" Knowings and "Jumpin'" Jackie Jackson (I spent a lot of time looking at the bottom of their sneakers). Also young Walt Simon, Ralph "The Durango Kid" Bacote (a rare and wondrous jump shooter), Eddie "The Czar" Simmons, Bob McCullough, and Bobby "Zorro" Hunter.

Then there was Freddie Crawford, who didn't shoot all that much, never approached scoring 50, but just played basketball. There may not have been any Rucker headlines for Freddie, but he did play 297 workman-like games in his five-year NBA career.

The one thing all these guys had in common was a high level of skill. This was also true of many others, who didn't have such recognizable names.

I really enjoyed playing in the Rucker. I was at the top of my game and my jumper was money. But best of all was connecting with so many wonderful guys.

Of course, I played much more often in Philly's Baker League (which I helped to establish). In the beginning we played on an outdoor court, we called ourselves the Twenty-Fifth and Diamond Summer League, and had only four teams:

The squad from West Philly was led by Guy Rodgers, Hal Lear, and Jay Norman.

From North Philly came Tee Parham and Russell Gordon.

John Chaney led the team from South Philly.

Sonny Hill and I teamed up for Southwest Philly. I once scored 66 points in an outdoor game, which I believe is still the single-game scoring record.

We played twice every week and wore different-colored mesh pullovers. The refs and scorekeepers were all neighborhood volunteers. Since we never charged admission, the stands were always full. Many beautiful girls also volunteered to bring the players towels and cold drinks.

The games were like neighborhood block parties.

Before long, we attracted sponsors who paid for uniforms and refs, new basketballs, and other game-time necessities. Sometimes NBA refs would work the games—Joey Crawford and Leroy Alexander come to mind. My team's sponsor was a bar called Mr. Silk's Third Base, whose motto was "You have to touch Third Base before you go home."

Charles Baker was an uncle of Hal Lear's, and was also the head of Philly's recreation department. So Hal made a pitch to his uncle to provide us with an indoor court: There would be no rainouts and the players would be less likely to suffer serious injuries. Shortly thereafter, the newly named "Baker League" began playing in the Moylan Recreation Center.

The Baker League regulars included some guys I had spent my growing years playing against. Past, current, and future NBAers like Wilt, Andy Johnson, Woody Sauldsberry, Tom Hoover, Walt Hazzard (who changed his name to Mahdi Abdul-Rahman), Wayne Hightower, Guy Rodgers, Hal Lear (albeit briefly), Wally Jones (who would change his name to Wali), and Hubie White.

I also played against or with several other guys who played in either the NBA or the ABA: Bill Bradley, Charlie Scott, Chet Walker, Mo Cheeks, Hal Greer, and Luke Jackson. After I hung up my sneakers, the Baker League continued to attract an incredible lineup of professional players: Rasheed Wallace, Earl Monroe, Eddie Mast, Jim Washington, Andre McCarter, Lionel Simmons, Fatty Taylor, Lewis Lloyd, Willie Sojourner, Mo Lucas, Darryl Dawkins, and Larry Cannon.

There were two other prominent players who competed in the Baker League: Johnny "Red Ball" Sample, a Hall of Fame–bound defensive back for the New York Jets. Timmy Brown, a Pro Bowl running back for the Philadelphia Eagles. They were both very good players, who ran with us in order to get in tip-top shape for their NFL training camps.

Thank you, Baker League.

Before both the Rucker and the Baker Leagues were established, I also played in several New York vs. Philadelphia All-Star games. Since Wilt was born in Philly and lived in New York, when he was playing with the Warriors, he always had his choice of which team he played for. And the team he picked always won.

However, one summer Wilt played for Philly, and although his team won, New York's Connie Hawkins was named the game's MVP. Another time when Wilt led New York to the win, Philadelphia's Tom Hoover was the game's MVP.

Overall, it was beautiful to watch both the Rucker and the Baker grow into important venues for talented players.

CHAPTER THREE

NOT SUCH A BIG MAN ON CAMPUS, THEN FAR EAST OF THE NBA

So, after playing at City Tech, I was off to Portland University on that three-day train ride. However, a few months later, in order to get to Philly and back during my brief Christmas break, I had to fly. I was just amazed and I stared out the window the whole time.

On my way back to Portland I found myself sitting next to Herb Adderley, buddy from our growing-up days. He was on his way back to Michigan State, where he was in his junior year. Herb, an outstanding running back with the Spartans, was also an outstanding baseball and basketball player. In my experience, Herb was the best all-around athlete to come out of Philly. However, when he was drafted by Green Bay, the Packers—with Jim Taylor, Paul Hornung, and Elijah Pitts—were loaded at that position. The legendary Vince Lombardi told Herb he had no chance of making the team as a running back. "Have you ever played defense?" Lombardi asked. "No," said Herb, "but I'll try." Eventually, Herb became a Hall of Fame cornerback. But these cards hadn't been dealt yet.

Herb and I said our goodbyes when he got off the plane during a brief stopover in Detroit. In those days, there were no stretch corridors, so I watched Herb battle his way through a fierce wind, shivering cold, and five inches of snow. I could see his coat flapping and I thought, "Detroit? This is definitely not for me. I'm happy to be headed for the sunshine."

And God laughed.

Both before and after I was there, several guys who eventually graduated into the NBA or the ABA played at UP. These include Darwin Cook, Bill "Slim" Garner, Jose Slaughter, Greg Anthony, Cincy Powell, and Eugene "Pooh" Jeter. Not to forget Erik Spoelstra, who's still coaching the Miami Heat.

Unfortunately, my transfer grades kept me from suiting up during my first semester at UP. I wound up playing in the final thirteen games of the 1957–58 season, averaging 20.3 points and 11.4 rebounds, and was an honorable-mention All-American.

Elgin Baylor was at Seattle University and I got to play against his team twice. The first time we were up by 17 at the half and I scored a bunch of points. It was clear that they had taken us lightly and thought they would just roll over us. But they woke up in the second half, including having a long-armed 6'10" guard me. He legally beat me up, bumping me and playing chest-to-chest defense. I wound up with 29 points, most of them in the first half, Elgin lit us up for 60, and we lost by only 1 point.

The second time we played Seattle, I managed 21 points against the same 6'10" guy, Elgin dropped 40, and we lost by 4.

So I still hadn't seen Elgin lose.

But trying to beat Elgin and Company was the least of my problems at Portland. My scholarship was withdrawn after I failed "Apologetics," and my grades fell below the required 2.0 index. That meant I had to find a job to pay my room and board.

The only one I could find was to work with a sledgehammer to help break down deserted buildings. An exhausting job, especially when it came to trying to break down a building's foundation.

So I thought that if I had to work that hard, I might as well go back home and find a job there. And that's what I did. When I returned to Philly, however, I was thrilled to discover that I didn't need a sledgehammer to earn a decent wage.

The blessed alternative that presented itself was the Eastern Professional Basketball League, a.k.a. the Eastern League (EBL). The games were played in and around Pennsylvania only on weekends and featured several incredible players. Guys like Dick Gaines, Wally Choice, Hal Lear, Roman "Doc" Turman, Stacey Arceneaux, Floyd Layne, Sherman White, Goose Powell, Ed Warner, Tommy Hemans, Boo Ellis, Sonny Hill, Bob Gainey, and the McCoy brothers. Because the NBA only fielded eight teams in those days, there simply wasn't enough room for these guys to graduate from the EBL.

It should be noted that all the great players listed above were African Americans. When I started playing in Allentown, both the NBA and the EBL fielded eight teams each, and the Eastern League had more Black players.

Sonny Hill was also (and still is) the dean of all things basketball in Philly. It was Sonny who arranged for me to join his team—the Allentown Jets—in the middle of the season. As I recall, I wound up playing fifteen games and averaging about 20 points and 10 rebounds, while getting paid $35 per game.

I came into the Eastern League as a somewhat raw player, simply because I never had any sustained periods of good coaching. So I owe a special debt of gratitude to Sonny Hill for spending time with me before and after games, helping me improve my crossovers, ball fakes, floor vision, defensive positioning, screen-setting, plus smoothing my shooting stroke.

Among my other teammates (both Black and white) who also took the time to help and encourage me were Brendan McCann, Pete Brennan, Doc Turman, Ed Burton, Gene Hudgins, and Art Spoelstra. I would also be ungrateful if I failed to thank several opponents for likewise supporting my efforts to improve my game—Carl Green, Jack Molinas, Stacey Arceneaux, Sherman White, and Hubie Brown. By the way, most basketball fans don't know that Hubie was a terrific player in the EBL. He was skillful, a good midrange shooter, smart enough to get the ball where it was supposed to go, and an outstanding defender. He averaged double figures, but what kept him from playing in the NBA was his lack of sufficient speed and quickness, plus his slender body.

I also learned by watching. Through it all, I made the transition to the pro game.

Playing the full 1959–60 season with the Jets, my numbers were 23.4 and 12.1, plus finishing as the third leading assist-maker with 4.5 points per game, and getting a $30-per-game raise. During my third and final season in Allentown I averaged 33.4 points and 16.4 rebounds, with my per-game salary raised to $85.

For sure, there were plenty of one-on-one players. However, there were so many experienced players in the league that, even without the benefit of charted X's and O's and without calling plays, we were also able to run disciplined, organized offenses.

Yet despite my personal success with the Jets, I was becoming increasingly ambivalent about my time in the Eastern League.

On the plus side: the league was much more important than I had initially realized because it broke down a lot of prejudices in small towns like Williamsport, Allentown, Wilkes-Barre, and Sunbury. The working people there previously had little or no contact with African Americans. But now they came to games, cheered for the African Americans on their home teams, and not only accepted us but often thought of us as heroes.

On the flip side: One evening during my first year with the team, the owner of the Allentown Jets invited Sonny Hill and me to dinner at his house. Also present were three of our white teammates. During the dinner, one of them said that he was feeling a bit chilly, so he left the table. From where I was sitting, I could see him climb the stairs, enter a bedroom, and pull a sweater out of a suitcase!

The three white guys were living there!

Meanwhile, my expenses over any given weekend included $10 for a bed in some fleabag motel, at least $25 for food, plus gas and tolls. So I was taking home maybe thirty bucks for two games.

I was hurt to the core by this.

Johnny Kimock was Allentown's public relations guy. He always encouraged me and also routinely sent my stats to all of the NBA teams, which was why I was scouted by three NBA officials: Red Holzman was a scout with the Knicks, Pep Martin was the general manager and vice president with the Cincinnati Royals, and Earl Lloyd scouted for the Pistons.

Holzman even invited me to a Knicks game at Madison Square Garden, where he introduced me to Fuzzy Levane, the team's coach. "Glad to meet you," said Levane. "Someday you could be a Knick."

Martin had a more promising comment: "We have the third pick in the upcoming draft and we're going to be looking at you."

And Earl Lloyd said this to me: "You're going to be our first pick." Then he turned to my mother, saying, "I'll take good care of him."

I was dubious about all their claims and promises. *Yeah, yeah,* I thought. *Words are easy. Actions are more difficult.*

What most of the EBL players and I felt was truthfully encouraging was the increasing number of Black players on NBA rosters. No longer would an African American player have to be a Wilt, a Russ, a "Big O," or an Elgin to make the league. Black players who were stars in college understood what they had to do to make their teams: become role players. And their teams greatly benefited by having extremely talented players coming off the bench. Here are some examples:

Shellie McMillon (Bradley) was a role player for the Pistons.

Willie Jones (Northwestern) also came off the bench for Detroit.

Sihugo Green (Duquesne) was a valuable sub for the St. Louis Hawks.

Al Attles (North Carolina A&T) played ferocious defense for the Philadelphia Warriors and then the San Francisco Warriors.

Tom "Satch" Sanders (NYU) made the Hall of Fame on the basis of the defense he played for the Celtics.

K.C. Jones (San Francisco) was another key defender for Boston.

"Jumpin'" Johnny Green (Michigan State) did his part-time elevating for several teams, including the Knicks.

Woody Sauldsberry (Texas Southern) could defend Elgin Baylor better than any of his peers while playing for Philly, St. Louis, Boston, and Chicago.

Ray Felix (LIU) was a scorer on the Lakers' second unit.

Andy Johnson (University of Portland) was a powerhouse role player for Philly

As for me, I initially went through the same process. When I was a rookie in Detroit, I went from scoring 33.4 points per game with the Allentown Jets to being primarily a rebounder and only incidentally a scorer. I was always an aggressive rebounder throughout my pro career, but my responsibility to put points on the board increased only when I became a starter.

However, because of my unique experience in the Eastern League, the transition was somewhat easier for me than for some of the other rookies. This was simply because I had already undergone a dynamic step up from college ball to the Eastern League in all aspects of the game.

As I've mentioned before, my NBA education was enhanced by Earl Lloyd, Dickie McGuire, and several others, but I also learned plenty just by sitting around in the locker room. I was never what might be called a "big personality," so I mostly listened as the veterans talked about how to play against certain players and teams and about which scouts and coaches were respected and which were not. It was extremely valuable front-line information.

Moreover, with the widespread coverage of the NBA by the media, there was a broad stream of useful information at my disposal. And I put everything I heard, saw, and read to good use.

I'll never forget the date—March 27, 1961. I was riding the subway on my way to a tournament in the Bronx. The NBA Draft had taken place that morning, so I was reading the *New York Post*, an afternoon paper . . . when I saw that . . . the Detroit Pistons had made me the fourth selection in the first round!

I let out a loud scream that startled all the other passengers!

Then, like a true veteran of subway riding, I quickly looked around, pretending that someone else had screamed.

WOW!

Earl Lloyd had told the truth!

But then I thought this:

Really? Me? Who only played a dozen games in college? Who was 6'9" but weighed only 215 pounds? Selected behind only Walt Bellamy by the newly enfranchised Chicago Packers; Tom Stith, a local guy picked by the Knicks, who was a terrific player hindered by lingering medical problems; and Larry Siegfried from Ohio State, selected by Cincinnati. Ahead of such future NBA and/or ABA stalwarts as Don Kojis, Bill Bridges, Kevin Loughery, Doug Moe, Tom Meschery, and Johnny Egan?

When Earl Lloyd and Dickie McGuire came to Fred Zollner, the owner of the Pistons, to express their desire to use their treasured first-draft pick on a guy from the EBL, this is what Mr. Zollner said: "Do what you think is right."

But, hey! Reality or fantasy! I was thrilled by and eager for the opportunity.

For sure, I was the fourth pick in the NBA Draft. Yet, coming from the Eastern League, I initially had no stature in the eyes of my new peers. Walt Bellamy had been the first pick and in our rookie 1961–62 season, he averaged 31.6 points and 19.0 rebounds per game. My numbers that initial season were 13.3 points and 11.5 rebounds—next to Bells's, the best of all the draft choices.

Thank you, Eastern League!

CHAPTER FOUR

ANOINTED BY THE DIPPER

On November 8, 1960, John Fitzgerald Kennedy was elected the thirty-fifth president of the United States. In his speeches, before and after this occasion, JFK's "New Frontier" signaled that African Americans could now be included in the American Dream. By themselves, JFK's words and the sentiments behind them improved the quality of lives for millions of people of color by encouraging us to feel better about who we were and what we could possibly achieve.

He didn't live long enough to legislate what he sought, so it was left to his successor, Vice President Lyndon Baines Johnson, to fulfill JFK's dreams.

Also, at the conclusion of the 1959–60 season, ninety-nine players appeared on the rosters of the eight NBA teams. Twenty-four of these players were African American, with the easy math coming to virtually 24 percent. However, subtracting the minuscule on-court time credited to the Celtics' Maurice King (who only played 19 minutes in a single game), and Cal Ramsey (who played four games in St. Louis and seven with New York), the meaningful number is reduced to slightly less than 22 percent. This percentage increased every year while

JFK was still in office, eventually reaching 38 percent in the year he was assassinated.

A huge step was also taken with the record number of African American players named to the 1964 Olympic team, which I believe had a great deal to do with the words and deeds of both JFK and LBJ. The 1960 team had only three Black players— Oscar Robertson, Bob Boozer, and Walt Bellamy. Four years later, Jim Barnes, Joe Caldwell, Walt Hazzard, Luke Jackson, and George Wilson constituted nearly half of the twelve-man squad.

This major change in the Olympics signaled a similar change in the NBA. In the subsequent 1964–65 season, 48.7 percent of NBA players were African Americans. This repre-sented an increase of 10.7 percent over the previous 1963–64 campaign.

Even so, the African American presence back in that 1959–60 season was particularly revealing and important. The Celtics were in the early stage of their dynasty, yet two franchises— Cincinnati and St. Louis—demonstrated their continued resistance to this new wave of outstanding players.

Here's a list of the total population at the time:

BOSTON: Bill Russell, K.C. Jones, Sam Jones, and Maurice King

CINCINNATI: Wayne Embry

DETROIT: Walter Dukes, Earl Lloyd, and Shellie McMillon

MINNEAPOLIS: Elgin Baylor, Alex "Boo" Ellis, Ray Felix, Ed Fleming, and Tom Hawkins

NEW YORK: Johnny Green, Willie Naulls, and Cal Ramsey

ST. LOUIS: Sihugo Green

SYRACUSE: Dick Barnett, Hal Greer, and Bob Hopkins

PHILADELPHIA: Andy Johnson, Guy Rodgers, Woody Sauldsberry, and the most impactful rookie in the history of the NBA—Wilt Chamberlain

I was fourteen when I first saw Wilt play. He was sixteen and already an amazing player at Overbrook High School back when the games consisted of four 8-minute quarters. He was 6′11″, 240 pounds at the time, and could run like the proverbial deer, jump out of the gym, and single-handedly prevented layups and short-jumpers on defense. At the other end of the court Wilt averaged well over 40 points per game, often scoring 60 or 70, with his high being 90. That's 90 points in 32 minutes!

Yet Wilt's offense didn't really develop during the three years he subsequently spent at the University of Kansas. In fact, it was while he spent one year with the Globetrotters that he developed his fadeaway bank shot that made him such a dynamic scorer when he got into the NBA.

In my junior year at West Philadelphia High School, we finished the season with a record of 17–3. We would have gone undefeated but for the three losses to Wilt's Overbrook dynasty. We seldom guarded each other, but he scored his usual 40-plus (and I was usually in foul trouble when he did), while I struggled to put up double figures.

My all-time favorite memory of Wilt took place when I was seventeen and riding my bike to the Haddington Recreation Center to see if there was anything happening on the basketball court. Wilt was nineteen, was playing at Kansas, and was already a much-celebrated All-American. I found him on the court engaged in a solo workout. I was thrilled when he invited me to join him. For what seemed like hours we shot, retrieved misses, passed to each other, and ran some sprints (when Wilt always left me behind).

After we were done, I was ready to bike my way back home, but Wilt had another idea. He put my bike in the trunk of his car and said, "I'm driving you home."

This meant a lot to me. He saw me as a real player but more importantly as a person. Indeed, his respect helped me to increase my own self-respect.

If I had to use one word to describe Wilt, it would be "complex."

Even if somebody my size—6′9″—walks into a room, "normal-sized" people stop, stare, and wonder who I am. It's really a unique experience always being the kid at the end of every size-place line. The one who has to be carefully placed in any group photo, who can't hide, and who is always the first suspect when something bad happens. Imagine how people reacted to the young Wilt.

How many times did he and the rest of us tall guys hear, "How's the weather up there?"

I believe that Wilt was essentially shy and very sensitive, and that he had to wear an outgoing, friendly face to protect himself in public.

Of course, even the most casual basketball fans know of Wilt's 100-point game, as well as the season when he averaged 50.4 points per game (1961–62). Over the course of his fourteen-year career, Wilt led the NBA in scoring seven times, in rebounding fourteen times, and even once in assists (1967–68).

The numbers are even more significant: Over the course of his twenty-year career, Kareem pulled down a total of 17,440 rebounds. Russ had 21,620 in thirteen seasons. For Wilt, it was 23,924 in fourteen seasons.

Then, in the 1967–68 season, Wilt led the league with 8.8 assists per game. Sometimes he'd come down with an offensive rebound but instead of easily dunking the ball, he'd pass to an open shooter—usually Hal Greer.

This last accomplishment revealed much about Wilt's mind-set. Along with his incredibly accurate fadeaway bank shot, Wilt's ability and willingness to make assist-passes were meant as proofs that instead of being a somewhat freakish high-scoring giant, he was a real and complete basketball player.

Too many fans and media were still not convinced, however. His oft-repeated quote reflected his continuing frustration: "Nobody loves Goliath."

Critics still unfavorably compare Wilt's winning only two championships to the eleven won by Bill Russell. The difference is simple: Russ played on much better teams, which featured a bevy of future Hall-of-Famers. These include Bob Cousy, Bill Sharman, Tom Heinsohn, K.C. and Sam Jones, John Havlicek, Satch Sanders, Bailey Howell, Frank Ramsey, Arnie Risen (briefly), Clyde Lovellette, as well as coach Red Auerbach.

When Wilt led Philly to a championship in 1967, the only other future Hall-of-Famers on the team were Hal Greer, Chet Walker, and Billy Cunningham. In winning the 1972 title with the Lakers, Wilt was assisted by Jerry West, the lone teammate to eventually be honored in Springfield.

Really. No matter how great a player is, he can't win a championship by himself. That's because basketball is a 5-on-5 team game.

In addition to his scoring heroics, Wilt was famous for his amazing strength, and I was able to witness one stunning example.

We were playing the San Francisco Warriors in the first game of a doubleheader in the old Madison Square Garden. After exchanging some words that I couldn't hear, Bob Ferry (6'8", 230 pounds) got into it with Al Attles (6'0", 175 pounds). There they were rolling around on the floor with Attles definitely beating hell out of Ferry, when Wilt suddenly approached. The ring of onlookers swiftly parted to let him through, whereupon he bent down, grabbed Ferry high on the arm with his right hand, grabbed Attles in a similar fashion with his left hand. . . . Then, as if it took no effort whatsoever, Wilt simply lifted both of them to their feet.

"That's enough," Wilt said, and it was so.

Everybody knew not to disagree with or even hesitate to agree with any directions Wilt ever delivered to anybody, in any place, about anything. If he told an opponent not to run out on defense and beat Wilt down the court, then we'd all slow up. If he told one of us not to execute a strategic off-the-ball foul on him, then we didn't.

Just how good was Wilt?

Since Russell was two years older and had already led Boston to a pair of NBA championships, Wilt admired Russ and tried to emulate him. He devoted increasing attention and energy to shot-blocking, rebounding, and passing. The first result of Wilt's evolution into fully accepting Russell's game plan was his leading the Philadelphia Warriors to a championship in 1967. He had perfected this transition by playing defense, like his respected rival, Russ, always did, and boosting a merely good 1971–72 Lakers team into a champion.

In truth, Wilt eventually mastered and even surpassed Russell's game plan, since he could still be the focus of his team's offense and could score points by the dozen.

Even late in his career, Wilt's defense was so exceptional that he was able to swat one of Kareem Abdul-Jabbar's "unblockable" Sky Hooks. Moreover, had Wilt been in his prime when Kareem came into the league, there was no way the youngster would have been able to deal with Dippy on either end of the court.

Here's an example of what Wilt could do when he felt he had to prove something: The expansion Chicago Packers made Walt Bellamy the top pick of the 1961 draft, and the first time Bells encountered Wilt was at a center jump.

"Mr. Chamberlain," said Bells with great deference as they extended their hands for the ceremonial shake. "My name is Walter Bellamy."

"I know who you are, Rook."

Wilt then proceeded to block Bellamy's first eight shots, after which he said this: "Okay, Rook. Now you can play."

Even as a rookie Bellamy was certainly no slouch. He averaged 31.6 points that season, and was eventually voted into the Hall of Fame.

There was another incident that we all knew about when "Jumpin'" Johnny Green scored a finger roll against Wilt, a shot that Wilt could easily have blocked. After Green scored, Wilt told him this: "Don't ever do that again. Because when I do block it, you'll break your wrist against the rim."

And Green thankfully obliged because, once again, a mere warning from Wilt was a total Stop sign.

Here's a statistic that also demonstrates Wilt's extraordinary endurance: In a combined total of regular-season and playoff appearances, he played in 1,210 games without ever fouling out. Moreover, with one notable exception (the seventh game of the 1969 championship series), he played every minute of every game. In fact, there were several seasons where, due to overtimes, he averaged over 48 minutes per game.

Also, there's no question that Wilt was the best all-around athlete ever to play in the NBA. That's because his undergraduate achievements in track and field were phenomenal—for example, running the hundred-yard dash in 11 seconds, high-jumping 6 feet 7 inches while wearing a cap and using the Western Role, which was soon to be eclipsed by the Fosbury Flop, a technique that added about five inches to the average jumper. And Wilt did this when the world's best were jumping 6 feet 11 inches. Moreover, Wilt ran the third fastest schoolboy 440 in Pennsylvania. Since pole vaulters could only use bamboo poles back then, Wilt was simply too big and too heavy to compete in this event, which was the only event that would have prevented Wilt from being an Olympian decathlon champion.

In the context of American culture Wilt Chamberlain was a national icon along with the likes of Babe Ruth, Red Grange, Joe Louis, and Jackie Robinson. And to many of his NBA peers, Wilt was held in the same regard.

I really don't like pontificating about who was the greatest player of all time, but I will say that my Mount Rushmore would feature George Mikan, Bill Russell, Wilt Chamberlain, and Kareem Abdul-Jabbar. That's because these players forced basketball to change its rules in its attempts to minimize their dominance.

Before Mikan, pivot men could plant themselves right at the basket, but to try to minimize Big George, a new rule was instituted creating a six-foot-wide lane and forbidding a player to linger there for more than three seconds. Early in Bill Russell's entrance into the NBA, the lane was widened to twelve feet. To keep Wilt away from the hoop, the lane was widened to sixteen feet—its current status. While Kareem was at UCLA, antidunking legislation was instituted. This actually worked in Kareem's favor, since he countered this ban by perfecting his Sky Hook.

For me, Wilt was the best of these other great centers. That's because he was skillful, played terrific defense, and could play with both power and finesse.

The only box that both Russ and Kareem left unchecked was "Power."

The second-tier centers include Shaq, who was all power and a minimal defender. Nate Thurmond, who played wonderful power defense. Walt Bellamy was all-finesse. Dave Cowens and Willis Reed weren't finesse guys and were too small to over-power bigger centers.

As Wilt's prominence and dominance increased both on and off the court, our relationship became more distant. For sure, we shook hands before our teams competed, and sometimes went to jazz clubs together in Philly or Detroit, but we were no longer home boys, because we were competitors.

Even so, I remember one summer day when we were both at Kutsher's to play in the Stokes Game. When Wilt, Carl Green, and I sat down for lunch, we wound up talking, reminiscing, and laughing for two hours. When we parted, Carl said this to me: "I love you, man." Then Wilt said, "I love you, too."

Back then, men didn't say that to each other, so I was stunned. I was thirty-five at the time, had known them for twenty-one years, and had no idea that they felt that way about me. And I've always kept what they said in my heart. Even now, I sometimes tear up whenever I think about it.

Then, in the winter of 1996, while I was recuperating from knee and shoulder surgery, Wilt made his periodic connection with Sonny Hill. When Sonny told Wilt about my situation, Wilt called me and we had a conversation that made me feel even closer to him than ever before. He asked about my wife and children, then said he'd been thinking about the fact that he'd never married and had no children. It was clear to me then that Wilt deeply regretted not having a family, and I think he never got over this particular sadness.

It wasn't, and still isn't, well known that Wilt gave a million dollars a year to establish and fund Operation Smile to provide cost-free corrective surgery to children in Third World countries who had been born with cleft lip and other facial impairments. The foundation remains well-funded and still presents an annual Wilt Chamberlain Humanitarian Award.

Ten years ago, long after my basketball career was in the rearview mirror, I was working as a development director for the Lutheran Child and Family Services of Michigan when Wilt's sisters, Barbara and Selina, called to say that before he passed, Wilt told them that he had personally wanted me to have this award.

This was one of the greatest thrills in my life.

As he had done when I was seventeen, my old Philly buddy was once again helping and honoring me, this time from his grave.

CHAPTER FIVE

A STRANGER IN PARADISE

I was a typical wide-eyed rookie with a lot to learn in my rookie NBA season of 1961–62. And my first lesson happened before I stepped onto the court.

I had just signed a two-year contract worth $25,000 (that's $219,922 in today's value) and was hanging out with Earl Lloyd in a room at the Sheraton. Because I knew every roadside motel from Philly to Allentown, I was impressed on several levels. Not the least of which was my signing bonus in the form of a $1,000 check, which I had in my pocket. We had just finished a wonderful meal in the dining room, but I was craving dessert.

"With this room-service deal," I asked Earl, "could I have some apple pie à la mode?"

Earl chuckled. "You're the number-one draft pick of this franchise, Ray. You can call and order whatever you want."

That's when it really hit me.

Man! I'm here! I have ARRIVED!

The start of the season taught me a much more meaningful lesson.

First of all, none of the players knew who I was or who I

was supposed to be. While they had been All-Somethings in college, I was a skinny kid from Allentown.

Allentown? Where the hell was that?

However, when I first joined the team I was met in the hotel lobby by Bailey Howell, who was born in Tennessee and was a graduate of Mississippi State. I was totally surprised (and appreciative) when he shook my hand and said, "Welcome, Ray. Glad to have you join us."

However, since I had been such a high-volume scorer in the Eastern League, I thought I'd have the same role with the Pistons. I really expected that I'd score about 20 points a game.

Nowadays, a team's first-round pick gets so much money, and there's so much riding on the efficacy (and continuing employment) of the team's scouting corps, that "the chosen one" has to get major minutes from the get-go. But back when I was a rookie, even first-round picks had to earn their playing time. So the exhibition season was when I had to prove that my presence on the floor could have a positive impact. But that was not the case when we played what is now called a "preseason game" against the Knicks.

Dickie McGuire was the Pistons' coach, and because he had been a stellar player with the Knicks, he really wanted to beat them. Unfortunately, my performance was a significant reason why his earnest wish didn't come true. That's because I was matched up against Willie Naulls, a seasoned veteran, who simply ate my lunch. I bought every one of his shifty fakes, was puzzled by his moves, and helplessly watched while he drained a seemingly endless number of midrange jumpers.

After the game, Dickie was on my case. "I told you to stay up on Naulls!"

He surely did, but there was a huge gap between his words and my actions.

We opened the season in the Boston Garden against the best team I'd ever seen. The Celtics started Bob Cousy, Bill Russell, Sam Jones, Tom "Satch" Sanders, and Tom Heinsohn. Plus they had Frank Ramsey and K.C. Jones off the bench.

Before the game, the latest NBA championship banner was raised, and the hometown heroes received their championship rings. Then they proceeded to stomp us into the mud. I started, but was similarly stomped by Heinsohn.

I played a starter's time—about 30 minutes—but I was more intent on hunting for my shots than creating any problems for anybody on defense.

So, after getting buried by Naulls and Heinsohn, it appeared that my negative evaluation was complete. But I did get another unexpected chance during our next game, which was the first-ever NBA game played in Cobo Hall. Our opponents were the Los Angeles Lakers, but George Lee started instead of me. So I sat on the bench and watched Elgin Baylor (there's that name again!) have his way with Lee. Back in the locker room, Dickie told me that I would be starting the second half.

However, even though I concentrated on loosening up, once the game started, I was running in mud. Before Dickie had a chance to yank me back to the bench, the Lakers had gone on a 10–0 run. For the next few weeks, I only played in blowouts.

That's when Earl Lloyd took me aside. He pointed out that the team's designated shooters and scorers were a trio of ex-All-Americans—Bailey Howell, Don Ohl, and Gene Shue. To emphasize this, Earl said that while the Pistons averaged about 100 points per game, these three put up 60 points. The Pistons wanted me to be in the rotation, but my job was to figure out what role I could play to help the team.

I decided that if the primary responsibility to shoot and score was not to be mine, I would focus on playing defense and especially on rebounding. As my defense improved, I was able to demonstrate in "garbage" time that I was a dominant rebounder. Besides scuffling on the boards, I ran, and made most of whatever open shots came my way. And that's how I earned my way back into prime-time game-time.

There was one time-out huddle that was still another epiphany. We were losing and Dickie started yelling, "What're you guys doing out there? Ray's busting it and getting us the rebounds and you guys are doing nothing!"

That's when I thought, *NOW I'm a pro!*

Turned out that I finished only behind Howell, and twelfth in the league, with 11.5 rebounds. Plus I managed to average 13.3 points. Not too bad, considering I had missed so many games early on. As a result, by midseason I was starting, something I did until 1969.

Because I had competed against so many great players, as my minutes increased, my shock at the level of competition I was facing decreased. I was matched up against great players like Elgin Baylor, Bob Pettit, Paul Arizin, Jack Twyman, and Tommy Heinsohn, but I was never intimidated.

For sure, I still had plenty to learn: One vital lesson was to become more aware of the rhythm of the game and the rhythm of the various teams. For example, some teams wanted to up-tempo their offense, while others slowed the game. Most of the better teams fed an impactful player in the low post—Wilt in Philly, Russ in Boston, Bells in Chicago, and Johnny Kerr in Syracuse. The idea being to initiate the offense by getting the ball as close to the hoop as possible.

Other teams made their forwards the focus of their offense—Bob Pettit in St. Louis, Elgin in Los Angeles, Dolph Schayes in Syracuse, and Howell in Detroit. The Knicks started the trend of posting up big guards, notably the incomparable Richie Guerin.

Among the other, more self-protective physical lessons I had to learn was how to navigate screens and picks when playing defense. A screen is a stand-still obstacle that a ball handler seeks to run his defender into. But a pick is when the obstacle seeks you out and runs into you.

Okay. I was told that, when setting either one, I should make sure that I dropped my hands to cover my privates. That's because guys like Arlen Bockhorn and Richie Guerin would use their elbows and knees to also attack the thighs of the screeners and pickers. But never the knees, nor were any drivers hit below their hips, because these "cheap shots" could easily end a player's career.

Yet the guys who vigorously attacked screens and picks were not considered to be dirty players. They were only classified as being "physical." The bigs who were asked to set these roadblocks were just careful to protect any parts of our bodies that were exposed. After a few too-close encounters with the practitioners of this bang-them-before-they bang-you tactic, this was a lesson that I learned very quickly.

I was a good student and gradually learned to make whatever adjustments and improvements were necessary. But, for the most part, good students come from good teachers. With all the traveling and downtime in hotels, I did a lot of reading. Writers like James Baldwin, Richard Wright, Alex Haley, Malcolm X, Ernest Hemingway, and Langston Hughes really helped to center me and become a better player and a better person in several ways: I became more aware of my heritage and was increasingly able to engage in the perpetual discussions of race with my teammates. Reading helped me to relax, an important part of conserving my energy during the long NBA seasons. At the same time, reading Hemingway stimulated both my imagination and my sense of adventure. Being better informed about so many things helped make my life more interesting. The sheer concentration that my reading required encouraged me to engage in a deeper study of basketball.

In the early 1960s, the owners had total control of the players. No beards or long hair were allowed, and we had to uphold a strict standard of professionalism. So since the men who attended the games wore jackets and neckties, we, too, had to dress like businessmen whenever we appeared in public.

Plus, if we happened to bring a girlfriend or wife to a game, they had to dress just like the women fans—as if they were attending cocktail parties.

Even as I absorbed these lessons, my NBA education included a particularly painful incident, which occurred during the training camp of my second season in Detroit.

Many players feel a connection with the number on their jerseys. It may be some sort of comfort level, or superstition, or a personal statement. Robert Parish wore #00, Wilt had #13, Dennis Rodman wore #90, and back in the dawn of the NBA George Mikan had #99. My favorite player, Elgin Baylor, wore #22. Having played against him in college and watched him on TV, I certainly admired his talent but, even more, I liked the way he conducted himself both on and off the court. With dignity, humility, and class. That's why, during my successful rookie season in Detroit my number was also 22.

Let me preface what happened by noting that I had personally witnessed Dave DeBusschere play at the University of Detroit. He was a 6'6", 220-pound, white guy whose remarkable skills covered both ends of the court. He could pass, shoot, handle, rebound, and above all play Velcro defense. I was therefore happy when the Pistons made him their top choice in the 1962 draft, because he'd certainly make us a better team.

I didn't take much notice that he wore #22.

Not only was DeBusschere a terrific hooper who was eventually bound for the Hall of Fame, but he was also a great baseball player. That's why, when the Pistons assembled for our team photo, Dave was absent-with-leave and pitching for the Chicago White Sox while, once again, wearing #22.

On the day we gathered for the taking of the Pistons' 1962–63 team photo, uniforms were handed out, and the number on the jersey given to me was #12. Where was *my* #22? It was eventually given to DeBusschere when he joined the team.

I was very upset.

At the time, management offered no explanation, no apologies, and no respect. Instead of just making a unilateral decision, they should at least have asked me about the change.

Anyway, I never spoke about this to Dave, because it had not been his decision. Even now, I'm still rankled by it all.

When I joined the Baltimore Bullets, Kevin Loughery already wore #22, so I never made a fuss and settled for #31. It wasn't until I played for the Virginia Squires in the ABA that I got to wear #22 again.

I certainly enjoyed playing with the best players in the world. Yet another source of enjoyment was traveling from city to city. Here's a twenty-two- or twenty-three-year-old's impression of every stop the Pistons made during my first two years in the NBA:

BOSTON: There was always a strong undercurrent of racism there. So whenever we had some free time, we'd have to figure out which were the restaurants, the movie theaters, and the nightclubs where we'd be welcome. And, conversely, which ones to avoid.

CHICAGO: All the visiting teams had to stay at a hotel that was near the stockyards. Especially when the wind was blowing, the smell was so bad that we ate in the hotel and stayed in as much as possible. It was also a hard place to play, because the games took place in multiple arenas, so we couldn't get comfortable with the different courts, baskets, and sight lines.

Even so, Chicago was the cultural bedrock of jazz, so on my own I explored the Loop, and went to several clubs. Among the jazz giants that I saw was the Miles Davis Quintet, which included John Coltrane, Wynton Kelly, Philly Joe Jones, and Paul Chambers.

That's why, despite the odor of butchered livestock, I always looked forward to coming to Chicago.

CINCINNATI: Because it was right across the river from Kentucky, being there was like being in the Deep South, forcing us to learn how to get around and where we could safely go. For us, the best of Cincy was the jazz clubs, where we could enjoy the likes of Richard "Groove" Holmes and Ray Bryant. Another plus was that Frank Robinson and Vada Pinson, two of the Cincinnati Reds' star players, lived in town and would always show up at our games. More often than not it seemed that they were the only African Americans in the arena. Their support and goodwill meant a lot to us.

DETROIT: Set at the riverfront, Cobo Hall was the newest arena in the league. It looked good, smelled good, plus the court and the sight lines were also good. And Detroit was a great city to navigate so long as you had a car. There were no subways, the bus service was erratic, but all the streets and byways were built to accommodate cars. Willie "The Bird" Jones and Earl Lloyd introduced me to a wonderful club—the 20 Grand—where I saw performances by Aretha Franklin, Marvin Gaye, the Four Tops, the Temptations, Les McCann, and Freda Payne.

Detroit was my adopted home and I loved living there and enjoying the "Union Town" experience. The efforts of the United Auto Workers Union had created a booming middle class in the Motor City.

LOS ANGELES: Playing there was a dream come true, and it was when the Lakers moved here from Minneapolis that the NBA became a big-time league. Stars playing among stars. We'd usually play two games there, arriving on a Tuesday, playing Wednesday and Saturday, then taking a red-eye to our next stop. So there was plenty of time for parties, where I was thrilled to meet people like Doris Day, Richard Boone, and Hugh O'Brian. I was now hanging out with people who had only been imaginary before.

I've always been a fan of boxing and during my stopovers in LA, I'd also get free tickets to see some terrific boxing matches. The best of these was seeing Archie Moore in his prime.

NEW YORK: We loved playing here, because we could go almost anywhere and do almost anything we wanted to. I say "almost" because there were still some Whites Only venues. The jazz clubs in Harlem and in Greenwich Village were especially great places—the Village Vanguard, the Red Rooster, Big

Wilt's Smalls Paradise, plus the bebop oriented clubs around Fifty-Second Street. It should be noted that the 1966–67 season was a critical one for the NBA because it's the year when Bill Bradley and Cazzie Russell were both drafted by the Knicks and signed equitable contracts. The celebrity of these two players harkened back to the widespread interest in the college game matching Bradley's Princeton Tigers and Russell's Michigan Wolverines at the 1966 Holiday Festival at Madison Square Garden. With these two playing in New York, the NBA now had national appeal. NBA games began to appear on national TV, and the league started making lots of money.

Previously, most of the NBA owners were promoters—Walter Brown, Ned Irish, Danny Biasone, Eddie Gottlieb, and so on. But with millions in profits now available, wealthy men like Jack Kent Cooke began buying franchises, and the NBA was on its way to becoming an unequaled success. Really, just look at the twenty-five-to-thirty-million-dollar annual contracts even many current role players get today.

PHILADELPHIA: My true hometown. Paul Arizin had played at Villanova and was a Philly legend. In my debut back home, I blocked his first shot. *What a thrill!* And Arizin was a super guy. Sometimes I'd see him in various places around the city and he was always encouraging, not only to me but to all the Black kids he met.

Eddie Gottlieb still ran the team, and he still wasn't very fond of African American players. In the team's first year in the BAA, Joe Fulks was a one-man offense, who led the league in scoring. Since Fulks was white, he was the epitome of Gotty's dream. Sure, he signed and promoted Wilt, but Gotty did so not because his prejudice had diminished but because he knew that Wilt would make him money. Above all, Gotty remained a promoter.

ST. LOUIS: For African Americans, this was the most dreaded place to play. The entire team stayed at the Sheraton, however, the dining room didn't open until five o'clock, an hour after we had to eat our pregame meal. So while the white guys ate in fancy restaurants, the rest of us had no other choice but a greasy spoon. Also, if anybody was greatly offended by being called the N-word during a game, then they couldn't play in St. Louis.

SYRACUSE: We watched more TV in this town than anywhere else in the league, simply because there was nowhere for anybody, Black or white, to go. Nowhere! So it was important to have a good roommate here, and I had plenty over the years— Willie "The Bird" Jones, Reggie Harding, Dave Bing, Leroy Ellis, Rod Thorn, and many others.

When the Philadelphia Warriors moved to San Francisco, and the NBA later expanded into Portland, Phoenix, Seattle, Charlotte, the teams in Florida, and other locations, my experience and appreciation of the league likewise expanded.

Although he was a transcendent player, I would be remiss if I failed to credit Oscar Robertson with all he has done off-the-court to benefit so many NBA players, NBA owners, and the entire league.

In the early 1960s, the NBA players formed a union, an organization that was not officially recognized by the league's board of governors. Then, one day in the summer of 1967, Oscar requested and was granted a meeting in Baltimore with the board in order to propose the certification of the union. This sought-after certification would make the owners legally obliged to honor everything written and duly signed in every player contract. Oscar had been diligently prepped beforehand by Larry Fleisher, a famous contract lawyer, but his owners would only permit Oscar and the players who had been elected to attend the meeting.

Since I represented the Bullets, I was also present. The other players included Walt Bellamy (New York), Don Nelson (Boston), Paul Silas (St. Louis), and Archie Clark (LA Lakers).

Sitting on the other side of the long table were a group who were among the most powerful men in sports. Their league was only twenty years old and was making more and more money for them with each passing season. At the time, the league had only nine teams, but the more money that was to be made by owning an NBA team, the easier it would be to attract other rich men and thereby to expand the league.

Among the owners on hand were Danny Biasone from Syracuse; Ben Kerner from St. Louis; Walter Brown, who owned the Celtics; Philadelphia's Eddie Gottlieb; Arnie Hoeft from Baltimore; and Jack Kent Cooke, who had recently purchased the Los Angeles Lakers. This was their world and we lived in it.

So, only two years after several major colleges were just starting to integrate their basketball teams, there was a Black man putting his career on the line before a jury of his league owners, representing over a hundred players, and putting forth a proposal that the players' union be certified by the board. Not showing a hint of being intimidated, and having been thoroughly briefed by Fleisher, Oscar spoke calmly, covering every possible detail and every possible objection.

In retrospect, I presume that since many of the owners ran other businesses, they most likely had to deal with labor unions and either the threat of strikes or actual ones. Perhaps they thought that calling for a strike if our proposal was denied was an option for us. If that did happen, the owners would certainly lose lots of money.

Anyway, this is my informed conjecture.

Whatever they were thinking, after listening to Oscar's presentation, the owners could have just refused the proposal. Instead, Jack Kent Cooke, obviously impressed, said this: "This is a well-presented group of young men." His peers nodded in agreement. . . .

And suddenly a small but significant part of the world changed right before my eyes.

In San Juan, Puerto Rico, during the late spring of 1970, a group of NBA functionaries officially certified the National Basketball Players Association (NBPA). I had recently been selected in the expansion draft by the Buffalo Braves, but I had not yet gone to Buffalo to discuss my own situation. However, since I was the only player present who was a member of a team that existed only on paper, I was on hand to act as the Braves' union rep. As such, I also cast one of the unanimous ballots that made Oscar the president of the new organization.

Oscar, then, was, almost single-handedly, the rising tide that lifted up the players and the entire league. That's why Oscar "Big O" Robertson ranks with the likes of Wilt Chamberlain, Bill Russell, Kareem Abdul-Jabbar, Michael Jordan, Larry Bird, and Magic Johnson as being among the most influential forces in the history of the NBA.

CHAPTER SIX

BLACK MAN OUT

Cleo Hill was from Winston-Salem State, where he played for Clarence "Big House" Gaines, a Hall of Fame coach, so he had a complete game. A solidly built, 6'1" leaper, Hill was quick as the wind, played excellent defense, shot jumpers and righty and lefty hooks, and was a superb one-on-one player.

Cleo hails from New Jersey, and I first connected with him on various playgrounds in and around Philly. He was a smaller version of Earl Monroe. I mean, he could PLAY.

Cleo's biggest problem was getting drafted by the St. Louis Hawks, so he was playing in a city that was as racially segregated as any place in Mississippi or Alabama. African Americans couldn't even eat in Stan Musial's restaurant. The owner of the Hawks, Ben Kerner, had traded the rights to Bill Russell to Boston because Russell wanted to be paid $20,000. Even worse, after leading the USA to the Gold Medals in the recent Melbourne Olympics, Russell wanted to rest, and would sit out the first half of the forthcoming NBA season.

So here was Cleo Hill, a kid from an all-Black college, thrown into a hostile environment.

He was chosen by the St. Louis Hawks as the eighth pick in the 1961 draft, which meant he was the next-to-last player selected in the first round. The disappointing consequence of that was the meager contract he was given. Being a first-round pick translated into being the eighth-best college player in America that year. So he was woefully undervalued by the $7,500 one-year no-cut contract he signed.

Right before the opening of the 1961–62 season, I was a team-mate of Cleo's in a game against the Knicks in Madison Square Garden. We were the College All-Stars as selected by the New York sportswriters, and I was added because I had been such a high draft pick. We were coached by Horace "Bones" McKinney from North Carolina State, and the team included, among others, Johnny Egan (Providence) and Dave Budd (Wake Forest).

The Knicks were paced by Willie Naulls, Richie Guerin, Johnny Green, and Phil Jordon.

I led the All-Stars with 22 points, and Egan had 20, but the experienced Knicks beat us. However, playing with Cleo gave me another look at his skills and convinced me that he had a future as an NBA All-Star.

Both of us were rookies in that 1961–62 season, and the Pistons went on to play the St. Louis Hawks a total of twelve times (winning seven). Playing against him that season did nothing to lessen my belief in Cleo's brilliance and his prospects of a bright future in the league.

However, Cleo's game did not fit with the way the Hawks played. Isolation players like him didn't need any help from his teammates in order to score. Plus, Cleo was at his best on the run.

At the time, the Celtics were the only NBA team whose offense was based on running. That's because Boston had Russ, Satch Sanders, K.C. Jones, Tom Heinsohn, Frank Ramsey, Bob Cousy, and Sam Jones. But Cleo's new teammates—Bob Pettit (LSU), Cliff Hagan (Kentucky), and Clyde Lovellette (Kansas)—had all come from colleges that had deliberate, slow-paced game plans and all-white teams and therefore had no interest in upping the pace. They were doing fine, so why change? After all, the year before Hill joined the Hawks, Bob Pettit averaged 27.9 points per game, Cliff Hagan 22.1, and Clyde Lovellette 22.0.

Lenny Wilkens was in the army. Shellie McMillon and Bobby Sims didn't join the Hawks until midseason, and both were role players. Besides Cleo, the only other Black player on the team when the season began was Fred LaCour, who was biracial.

So Cleo Hill was rejected on two counts—for the color of his skin, and for the particular nature of his outstanding talents.

Paul Seymour was the coach and a supporter of Hill. In the fourteen games he played under Seymour, Cleo recorded 28 minutes, 10.8 points, 5.5 rebounds, and 2.3 assists per game while shooting 36 percent. Then Seymour was fired and replaced by Fuzzy Levane for sixty games, who was then succeeded by Pettit for six games. Under Levane and Pettit, Cleo averaged 15 minutes, 4.1 points, 2.4 rebounds, and 1.9 assists while shooting 34 percent.

On September 11, 1962, the day before training camp opened, Hill was cut and never signed by another NBA team. So he wound up in the Eastern League. From 1963 to 1967, he played a total of 101 games with the Trenton Colonials and then the New Haven Elms, averaging 15.5 points, 3.4 rebounds, and 3.1 assists per game. Despite his impressive numbers, Cleo's unjust banishment from the NBA really affected him. Guys who played against him there said that he lacked a certain spark that he'd shown with the Hawks.

Cleo Hill's story is just one example of the countless tragedies in which untold numbers of Black men were prevented from totally manifesting their God-given talents. The more life experience I had, the more I came to realize that the basic reason these tragedies are everyday occurrences is that too many white Americans feel entitled to exert total control of the social and cultural environment.

CHAPTER SEVEN

IN THESE CHANGING TIMES

Even with a strange number on my chest and on my back, I still had a very successful career with the Pistons. Throughout the next six seasons, I averaged a low of 15.5 to a high of 17.9 ppg, and in 1965–66 I led Detroit in assists. I played forward and sometimes dropped into the low post. And I worked constantly on my game, particularly my shooting. Indeed, over my nine years in the NBA my free-throw percentage increased from 63 percent to 80 percent.

One of my teammates during my rookie year was Chuck Noble. He was a seven-year NBA veteran and greatly encouraged me. "Ray," he said, "you can play." Those words meant everything to me.

The coach was Dickie McGuire, a New Yorker who had played first at St. Johns and then with the Knicks. Dickie treated all of us as individuals. He knew where we were born, what college we went to, and the names of the married players' wives.

In the 1962–63 season, Tom Meschery averaged 16.0 points and 9.7 rebounds, while Rudy LaRusso's numbers were 12.3 points and 9.9 boards. They were both terrific players and certainly deserved to make the All-Star team. I wound up averaging 16.2 points and 10.2 rebounds, and Dickie told me that I, too, deserved to make that team.

The support of a player's coach is incredibly important. With the encouragement of Dickie and Chuck Noble, I knew, at age twenty-four, that I was an authentic, productive NBA player.

We were a very harmonious outfit, as indicated by the card games we played whenever we flew. From the moment we took off to the moment we landed there were always two card games under way—blackjack and poker. I spent my rookie year reading books on flights, but there was so much laughter going on around both games that I eventually ended up with the blackjack group. Dickie was a permanent poker player, and it was another sign of our togetherness that our coach joined the players' games. In fact, Johnny Egan was the only one who didn't play, choosing instead to spend his time busting everybody's chops.

McGuire resigned after we went 34–48 in 1963–64, choosing to return to New York and be with his family. Under Dickie, Earl Lloyd had been an assistant coach and also Detroit's chief scout. Charles Wolf replaced Dickie, and Earl was relieved of his duties as assistant coach. Under Wolf our record was even worse—23–57—and he was fired after starting the 1964–65 season at 2–9. The natural, logical choice to succeed Wolf was Earl, since he knew Detroit's game down to every X and O and was popular with the players.

However, there were no Black coaches in the league. So, in what was probably a cruel and clumsy way to soften any disappointment that Earl might have felt, the team's general manager told him that had he been white, he could have replaced Wolf.

Instead, the twenty-four-year-old Dave DeBusschere became player-coach because he was perceived within the organization as being ultra-intelligent and having the wherewithal to succeed as a tactician, as well as having the ability to make personnel decisions.

As a young coach, Dave moved to create his own staff. Donnis Butcher was asked to retire in order to become his assistant. And I was named the team's captain. As a result, over a few beers after games and after practices, Dave frequently consulted us about things like potential trades, the apportioning of playing time, and the evaluation of players. We had a mutual respect, and since I was only twenty-six at the time, I greatly appreciated his interest in my views.

We finished out that 1964–65 season with Dave in command at 29–40.

However, our relationship changed midway through the 1965–66 season, when the Pistons made a trade that was news to me—dealing Rod Thorn and Joe Caldwell to St. Louis for Chico Vaughn, John Tresvant, and John Barnhill. This was a clear indication that my opinions were no longer being considered and that I was totally out of the loop.

The 1966 draft itself created another difficulty for me.

The Pistons (22–58) in the West and the Knicks (30–50) in the East finished with the worst records in their respective divisions. In order to discourage a team from tanking games to increase their chances of having the first pick in any forthcoming draft, the current rule mandated a coin toss to determine who would get this coveted option. The Pistons were eager to draft Cazzie Russell, who had starred at Michigan, but when New York in the East won the toss, the Knicks chose Russell. The Pistons then tabbed Dave Bing, a high-scoring guard from Syracuse. Dorie Murrey, from the University of Detroit, was the Pistons' second-round selection (eleventh overall).

In May 1966, Barnhill was picked by Chicago in the latest expansion draft. So as the Pistons' 1966–67 season got under way, the starters were Bing and Eddie Miles in the backcourt, with DeBusschere, Joe Strawder, and me up front. On the bench were Tom Van Arsdale, Ron Reed, Murrey, Don Kojis, Bill Buntin, Tresvant, Reggie Harding, and Vaughn. Yet the sense of harmony that the players had previously enjoyed was gone and we had difficulty trying to create a team identity.

Another problem occurred because Vaughn was stuck behind Bing, Miles, and Van Arsdale and wasn't getting enough minutes to get his game together. As a result, he was mostly bench-bound and was eventually cut in midseason. Chico was a terrific player, who quickly signed with the Pittsburgh Pipers and was instrumental in helping them to win the initial ABA championship.

With both Barnhill and Vaughn elsewhere, Dave chose to share my playing time with Tresvant. Plus, with Bing and Miles being top-notch scorers, they became the focus of our offense.

It didn't take long for all of these changes to affect me. We were overloaded with forwards, and with my minutes diminished, my confidence likewise diminished and I felt uncomfortable on the court. As a result, I was not at the top of my game, averaging only 14.7 points and 9.0 rebounds in the season's initial forty-five games.

I still loved living in Detroit, and playing in the NBA along with the very best athletes in the world. I dared to think that I would finish my playing days with the Pistons. At the same time, I had the distinct feeling that I could be traded at any moment.

PART TWO

CHAPTER EIGHT

LOOKING BACK

The journey of my life has benefited from the friendship, counsel, encouragement, and honesty of several people. In retrospect, it's clear that the most influential of these was Earl Lloyd.

On February 19, 1948, the Harlem Globetrotters played the game straight and upset the Minneapolis Lakers. George Mikan was acknowledged to be the best player in the game, and he had just led the Lakers to the championship of the National Basketball League (NBL). The Globetrotters then beat the Lakers again a year later. These surprising victories demonstrated that African American players could compete successfully at any level.

Shortly thereafter, Chuck Cooper from Duquesne was picked by Boston in the second round of the 1950 draft, becoming the first African American player ever drafted by an NBA team. Earl lasted until the Washington Capitols selected him in the ninth round, making him the first player from HBCU to be drafted. Moreover, on October 31, 1950, Earl also became the first Black player to appear in an NBA game. He scored only 6 points, but played tough defense and took down 7 rebounds.

During that game it chanced that a fan of the hometown

Caps was sitting right in front of a woman who, unbeknownst to him, was Earl's mother. As Earl checked into the game, the fan turned around with a question for the Black lady: "I wonder if that N-word can play?"

After Earl's solid performance, Mrs. Lloyd had the answer: "Yes, that N-word can play."

However, Earl only played in seven games before he was drafted into the army, where he served for the next two years.

Meanwhile, in the summer of 1950, the Knicks paid the Harlem Globetrotters $12,500 (the equivalent of $139,624 in 2021) for the contract of Nathaniel "Sweetwater" Clifton. Sweets was given $2,500 of the transaction and made his debut with New York on November 3, 1950. He proved to be a lockdown defender and robust rebounder.

By the time Earl was honorably discharged, the Washington Caps had folded and, in a dispersal draft, his rights belonged to the Syracuse Nationals. Earl was paired in the frontcourt with Dolph "Dolly" Schayes, and his job was to rebound, set picks, and guard the opponent's best forward. These days, Earl's responsibilities would define him as a "role player"; back then he was categorized as a "professional player."

In 1955, Earl and the irrepressible Jim Tucker became the first African American players to earn championship rings, when Syracuse beat the Fort Wayne Pistons in the seventh game of the NBA Finals.

Earl wound up playing with Syracuse and Detroit during his nine years in the league. He played his last game with the Pistons in the 1959–60 season before a series of injuries forced him to hang up his sneakers. Earl's lifetime numbers are 8.4 points and 6.4 rebounds per game, but it should also be noted that during his entire career, he missed only twenty-one games.

At the time of Earl's retirement, Mr. Fred Zollner was the Pistons' owner and Dickie McGuire was the team's head coach. Mr. Zollner and Dickie didn't waste a single beat in agreeing to make Earl the NBA's first Black scout. Before long, Earl also became the league's first Black assistant coach.

It was in early 1961, on one of his scouting expeditions, that Earl happened to meet Red Auerbach in an airport. A meeting that had a profound impact on my life.

During their conversation, Auerbach revealed that the Celtics were planning to draft a 6′9″ player named Ray Scott whom he had coached at Kutsher's, and who was currently playing in the Eastern League. Earl thought that if such a celebrated judge of talent was interested in this player, then he should take a look at this Ray Scott for himself.

Shortly thereafter, Earl arrived in Philly and came to my house to meet me and my family. This was a complete surprise, because NBA organizations normally spoke to players they were interested in drafting on college campuses. So I was greatly impressed with Earl's going above and beyond this tradition.

Then the two of us drove to Allentown for my next game. I was only twenty-two and Earl was a one-man NBA encyclopedia, an extraordinarily intelligent man, and superfriendly, so I must have asked him a thousand questions.

What's it like defending Elgin Baylor?

Is Oscar Robertson as good as everybody says he is?

Was Maurice Stokes that good?

How about some of the other players in the league? Wally Dukes, Rudy LaRusso, Sweets Clifton, Paul Arizin, Jerry West, Bob Cousy, Wilt, Russ, and on and on.

After witnessing the game, Lloyd said, "I like the way you

play, Raymond. We're gonna make you our number-one pick."
Which they did.

That's how and why Earl became my mentor and confidant.

Both Earl and Jim Tucker (who was my teammate with the
Allentown Jets) set the standard of behavior for Black players.
They were always respectful, honest, and conducted themselves
with dignity.

When I joined the Pistons, here are some of the other things
that Earl taught me about becoming an NBA player:

Where to eat and what to eat to maintain a proper diet.

To eat a pregame meal four hours before game-time. And in
order to provide a high delivery of protein, to always eat steak
and enough carbs for good energy.

Since no teams employed condition coaches, Earl taught me
to jump rope and do sit-ups and push-ups to stay in game condition—all of which I soon did on my own both during the
season and during the summers.

I also learned how to hail a cab in New York City. Trying to flag
one down while standing alone was a tough situation for a Black
man, especially one my size. The best bet was to stand in line along
with white people at an airport or a bus terminal. If that was impos-
sible, then I would walk to the nearest hotel, give the doorman a tip,
and he'd have an easy time flagging down a cab for me.

On the court, he taught me defensive spacing, the most
important points being not to let my man drive baseline but
instead pushing him to the middle, where the bigs' help would
be. I also learned how to move my feet and the proper hand-
checking technique—which was an apparent light hand on an
opponent's hip that was actually very forceful.

Above all, Earl said, "Work hard, Ray, and it'll all come to you."

I could also talk to Earl about personal issues. Like everybody else, I would complain to my assistant coach about my playing time.

I remember one night in Detroit when my legs simply weren't there. Something that occasionally happens during the normal marathon NBA season. And whenever I tried to quickly pivot or change direction, I wound up falling.

When Dickie yanked me from the game, I immediately complained to Earl. "Why did he take me out?"

"Because," Earl said, "you were flopping all over the floor like Bozo the Clown. So go sit down."

We both laughed.

So Earl was my big brother, and I did whatever he told me to do.

It was also Earl who gave me what was one of the greatest thrills of my life. This happened in my rookie season with Detroit, when we were at Newark Airport walking through a passageway leading to a plane we were about to board. We saw a group of Black men coming toward us. I was beside Earl and I recognized one of the men.

"Hey, Earl! That's Dr. Martin Luther King!"

He was beginning to appear on national TV because of the Montgomery bus boycott and for his activity in a voter-registration drive in the South.

Now, I knew that Earl was heavily involved in several of the current civil rights organizations, but I was surprised when he and Dr. King stopped when they came up to each other. I was even more surprised when Earl extended his right hand for a shake and said, "Hey, Doc. So good to see you."

They chatted for a few minutes, bouncing similar questions off each other.

"How've you been? . . . Where are you headed? . . . Any important victories? . . . Losses?"

Earl then said, "I want you to meet Ray Scott. I think he has a really good future in the NBA."

So I was also invited to shake hands with Dr. King. He was only about 5′9″, but he exuded a force that I felt but was too young to fully understand.

Years later, I was able to define what I had felt. It was the power of personal rectitude. Of goodwill. Of courage.

But at the time all I could identify was the physical power of his handshake.

Flustered, all I could think of to say was, "How are you?"

His answer was, "I'm tired. Really tired."

Since Earl and I were bringing up the rear, my teammates were too far ahead of us to be introduced. The whole conversation lasted only a few minutes, but I still cherish it.

CHAPTER NINE

CIVIL RIGHTS AND UN-CIVIL WRONGS

As America got deeper into the 1960s, everything seemed to change.

In music, pop artists like Perry Como and Patti Page, and TV shows like *Your Hit Parade* were passé. They were being replaced by Bob Dylan, Sly and the Family Stone, Joan Baez, the Grateful Dead, Jimi Hendrix, the Rolling Stones, Chicago, the Beatles, and others. In August 1969, Woodstock was the pinnacle.

And then there was Motown.

Songs now had meaningful messages, for example, James Brown's "Say It Loud, I'm Black and I'm Proud."

In film, traditional Hollywood romances and tearjerkers appealed to fewer and fewer moviegoers. The rage was for controversial films like *Easy Rider* and *Billy Jack*. Moreover, whereas audiences used to break into applause at the end of a movie, a stunned, thoughtful silence now prevailed as the credits rolled and were studied.

In 1966, I went on the first of my State Department overseas tours. The other African American participants were Bill Bridges, Wayne

Embry, and Al Attles. Don Kojis, Odie Smith, and Gene Tormohlen were my other teammates, but the leader of this pack was Richie Guerin, who was one of the toughest men I've ever met. He was 6′4″, 195 pounds, and, over the course of his NBA career, never backed down from anybody. There was one noteworthy incident when Richie got into a rumble with Andy Johnson, who was 6′5″, 240 pounds, and *the* toughest guy I ever played against. Punches were thrown and blood flowed until the fight was broken up.

Richie had been a Marine in his younger days, a player-coach for the St. Louis Hawks during the previous two years, and had a certain air of command about him. So it seemed to be predestined that Richie simply took over the show. As soon as we got off the plane, in Uruguay, a uniformed official approached him, saluted, and handed him our itinerary. Richie looked at the list and said, "We're not doing this, this, and this."

And we didn't.

We approached our first game with a laid-back, friendly attitude that resulted in a 10-point win. But the next day we were summoned to see the American envoy. This guy chewed us out, saying we had embarrassed our country. As a result, we started playing NBA basketball—making backdoor cuts, setting hard screens, playing chest-to-chest defense, and dunking whenever we could. We won our second game by 43 points, and similarly routed every other team we played.

I mean, we were ferocious! So much so that in one game Wayne Embry suffered something that he'd never experienced in the NBA—a bloody nose.

An envoy of the US State Department always sat behind our bench. After one of our wipeouts, Richie turned to the same guy that had chewed him out after the first game and said, "Are you satisfied now?"

The same lopsided margins were duplicated when we went to Brazil. But there was a much more significant situation that was present in both countries.

While the white citizens were virtually all very wealthy, the vast majority of indigenous Índios (or Charrúa) and Africans were living in abject poverty. Even though we were treated royally, when we went into the backcountry to do clinics, we despaired at the run-down shacks, starving half-naked children, and worn-out people we saw.

It brought home to us something that we had known about but never witnessed firsthand before—that racism is not confined to America.

More and more, the protests against the war in Vietnam showed the social and political divide in the country. It was interesting to note that during these protests it was mostly white kids who were being brutalized by the police, when not too long before it was mostly Black kids who were being assaulted in the civil rights protests. I think that the aggressive, negative reactions of older generations of Americans to both of these movements helped to show America the kind of country we didn't want to be.

In an attempt, perhaps, to change this perception of racism and intolerance at home, in 1968 the State Department sent Earl Monroe, Bob Ferry and me on a tour of military hospitals in the Far East.

Sending the three of us meant there would be a wonderful combination of personalities: Monroe and Ferry were always a pleasure to be around. They had a way of enjoying themselves in any circumstance, and their celebration of life was contagious.

We visited hospitals in the Philippines, Okinawa, Guam,

Taiwan, and Tokyo. It was heartbreaking to see so many young men who had suffered serious wounds fighting in Vietnam.

I had to put my finger over a hole in one man's throat to hear his voice.

Because the number of antiwar demonstrations back in the States was increasing, our job was to be supportive. In fact, we listened more than we talked. No matter how serious their conditions were, they all had one wish: "Get me back to the world." By this, they meant going back to America.

I was thirty at the time and was against the war. After reading whatever I could about the history of Vietnam and how most recently the French had failed to conquer the country, it was clear that no foreign country had ever won a war there.

I was encouraged, though, because the demand for racial equality became more and more public. Partially because of groups like the Black Panthers, and certainly because of the emergence of people like Martin Luther King and Malcolm X, the culture of America was being reshaped by voices that had never been heard so widely before on national public platforms. Voices against the war and against racism, and even some of the enormous financial power players were seeking to bend our country toward justice on virtually every piece of legislation.

If poor people and African Americans still weren't seated at the table, we were at least on the menu.

I also had some prior history with Bob Ferry. Long before we were on the State Department mission together, he had been a teammate of mine during my first few years in Detroit. Years later, when I was with Baltimore and he was an assistant coach there, we were flying on our way to begin a playoff series with the Knicks, when I said this to Ferry: "What a big and strong guy Willis Reed is."

That's when Bob give me some extremely important advice that, even though I had been in the league for several years, helped make me a better player. "Don't worry about Reed. You're big and strong, too. You don't realize how good you are, Ray, but sometimes you think too much. Just go out there and play."

The Black Panthers were an interesting organization. They instituted operations that greatly enhanced the lives of African Americans who lived in poor neighborhoods:

They set up and staffed free health clinics.

They fed preschool kids breakfasts.

They taught classes in self-defense.

They delivered groceries to the elderly.

They started a free school.

They provided a physical presence to protect their communities.

They started a nutritional program for young mothers and their babies. This program eventually became the federally funded Women, Infants, and Children Resource System, which continued to have the same function.

There was another action that about thirty Black Panthers took in Oakland: standing on the steps of a government building holding firearms. They did nothing to prevent anyone from either entering or leaving the building. Their only object was to demonstrate African Americans' desire and capacity for self-reliance. And we all know how many of these benefactors and brave protectors of the Black community wound up getting assassinated by the government.

As I've previously noted, my interest in racial justice had been informed by the trip to our nation's capital when I was much younger. But it was made even more powerful by my meeting with Dr. King, Malcolm, and also by an earlier connection with Muhammad Ali.

In 1964, Malcolm X had opened a mosque in Detroit near where I lived. The Champ had just attended a service at the mosque. I was driving to my apartment when I noticed Ali standing in front of the building with five or six people clustered around him. I parked, got out of the car, and walked over. I was just intending to see the Champ in the flesh, but he pointed at me and shouted, "I know you! You're the basketball player!" I mean he was jumping up and down with an arm extended like he was competing for a center jump. Then he laughed, saying, "I'll bet I can outjump you!"

After we shook hands, he invited me to accompany him to a TV station, where he was giving an interview. We wound up spending several hours together getting to know each other. I had just started promoting boxing cards, so we had a lot to talk about. This was the beginning of a long-term, very close friendship with him.

When we both happened to be in Detroit, he invited me to parties with guys like Joe Louis and Sugar Ray Robinson, among others. And we had many one-on-one private talks about the usual things—our families, the civil rights protests, game/fight preparations, and the cities we both knew.

Ali was a big guy—6′3″, 210 when he started, and 225 when he made his comeback after being suspended. Plus he was country-strong and had the wingspan of someone 6′9″.

There were two opponents that Ali really didn't like. Ernie Terrell and Floyd Patterson, and both for the same reason: Refusing to call him Muhammad Ali, they always referred to him as Cassius Clay. Instead of quickly knocking them down and out (which he could have done), he jacked them up, keeping them on their feet while he simply battered them bloody.

I was with Ali before the first Joe Frazier fight. I also knew "Smokin" Joe since he was also a Philly guy, and he was one of the friendliest people I have ever met. I had seen him fight several times, so I had his game plan down pat. He was only 5′9″ and 205 pounds in a big man's game so, for Joe, beating taller, tough guys was like chopping down trees.

Knowing Joe's moves so well, I shared what I saw with the Champ. "He's going to come at you much faster than you think. Much faster than you can move backward. Always looking to roll his shoulders to launch hooks that hit you from your blind side. He's also got a low center of gravity, so he can get under your punches." And so on. But the Champ didn't want to hear this. He just started shadowboxing and throwing incredibly quick punches. "Bam! Bam! Bam! I'm gonna knock him down! He's too small to hurt me."

As he usually did, the Champ would humiliate opponents by calling them names. He wanted to challenge their humanity, try to make them feel inferior to him. But Frazier was initially confused. I had heard that at the time Ali was suspended, both men lived in Philly, and Frazier would sometimes give Muhammad Ali money and drive him around. But now, Ali was talking down to Joe. "Why is he doing this?" Joe said. "Calling me those names. There's no pay-TV, all the tickets are sold, and we've already gotten paid."

It was a bad idea to antagonize Joe. He was a good man who had grown up in the hard-times South. When he arrived in Philly, Joe worked in low-wage jobs, such as in a meat processing plant, which made him tough and resilient. He also kept in shape by punching sides of beef as well as running through the streets of Philly. To my mind, what Joe had to go through in order to succeed as he did made him beyond admirable.

However, now Joe's mood turned from confusion to anger. I mean, Frazier didn't just want to beat the Champ, he literally wanted to destroy him!

Immediately after their third fight, Frazier's son Marvis came into his father's dressing room to say, "Ali told me to tell you that he's sorry for those things he said about you."

But Joe was still too deeply hurt by Ali's name-calling and said, "I won't accept his apology until I hear it directly from him."

And the hurt lingered.

However, late in his life, Ali did apologize to Joe face-to-face, and I pray that Frazier forgave him.

I think Ali made a mistake by trying to resurrect his career. He had gained too much weight and lost his quickness both in his hands and in his feet. As a result, he suffered dreadful beatings by Frazier, Larry Holmes, George Foreman, and Trevor Berbick.

But I believe that Ali wanted to show the world that he was not just a pretty boy. Like most boxers, he just loved to fight and punch people. That's why they call themselves fighters. Their motto is "I can take it." When they get hit, they believe that their next punch will hurt the other guy more than his punch hurt them.

I had two late meetings with Ali that both surprised me.

I was playing with the Virginia Squires in the ABA and we were in Miami for a game against the Floridians. Ali was also in town training for his upcoming fight against Jerry Quarry, and someone from his entourage called to invite me to the gym and say hello. But when I told my teammates that I was going to meet Ali, they freaked out. Especially Roland "Fatty"

Taylor, who said, "Man, you don't know Ali. You only wish you did."

Okay, so Fatty, Neil Johnson, Mike Maloy, and George Carter insisted on accompanying me. No problem.

Ali was in the ring getting toweled down by Angelo Dundee when four "giants" entered the gym. Dundee pointed to us and alerted Ali to our presence.

Ali then said something that astounded my teammates: "And Muhammad Ali knocked out Ray Scott!" And he came over and started shadowboxing with me.

This was in 1970, after I hadn't seen him in four years. What amazed me was how—although he must have met a million people during his career—he still honored me the way he did, recognizing me and instantly resuming our friendship.

Sixteen years later, when I was living in Detroit and working for an insurance company, the phone rang. It was Ali saying that he was in town at Curry's Barbershop in an African American neighborhood. So I drove there to meet him.

He was retired and we had a chance to catch up on what we'd both been doing since 1970. At the same time, there were lots of kids lined up to meet him. He gave each of them personal attention, shadowboxing with the boys and hugging all the little girls.

That was the last time I ever saw him.

I can honestly say that Muhammad Ali was one of the nicest, friendliest guys I have ever met.

My interest in the fight game predated my connection with Ali by several years.

I always thought of my stepdad, Sylvester Scott, as my father. (I didn't know that he had adopted me until years later, when I saw the information in the family Bible.) He was a devout boxing fan. And every Friday night at ten o'clock *The Gillette Cavalcade of Sports* would present radio broadcasts of boxing bouts. I slept on a Murphy bed, so starting when I was a four-year-old, I would sit with him and together we would listen to the descriptions of fights involving the likes of Kid Gavilán, "Two Ton" Tony Galento, "Sugar" Ray Robinson, and Joe Louis.

I was eight when he died, but I continued listening to the radio broadcasts. Later, when the fights were televised, my aunt Marie Bonaparte had a TV, and she let me come downstairs to her apartment to watch them.

Fast forward nineteen years . . . I was playing with the Pistons and was also the president, the matchmaker, and one of the founders of the Sportsmen's Boxing Club. During the off-season months, I was the primary organizer of several boxing programs that were held in Cobo Hall.

The fighters on these cards included:

Ron Harris, who had won a Bronze Medal in the 1964 Olympics. He was a diminutive, classy boxer.

Hedgemon Lewis, a native of Detroit, who had twice fought future Hall of Famer José Nápoles for the welterweight title. While Hedgemon didn't win, he fought well enough to make Detroit proud.

Alvin "Blue" Lewis, a heavyweight who faced Ali in Ireland early in the Champ's comeback. Lewis gave Ali all he could handle, and later became one of the Champ's regular sparring partners. During one of my promotions, Ali went three rounds with Lewis.

In all, I promoted six programs. The last one featured a bout between Boston Jacobs and George Chuvalo. Having fought Floyd Patterson, Joe Frazier, George Foreman, and gone the distance in two fights with Ali, Chuvalo was the main attraction and drew a large crowd. The ref was Willie Pep, who had fought in 241 fights in his twenty-six-year career and was the featherweight champ in the 1940s. When Chuvalo floored Jacobs early in the fight, Pep immediately signaled that the fight was over without bothering to start his count. The crowd went crazy, feeling deprived of the full action they had paid to see. But when I made a strong protest to Pep, he quickly and rudely blew me off.

My brief meeting with Malcolm X happened at 22 West, a restaurant on 135th Street and Fifth Avenue that was one of the safest places in Harlem for Black Muslims. I was passing by when I saw that he was inside, so I entered the restaurant and approached him. I could see several of his bodyguards there, but they were barely noticeable, casually sitting at tables, and made no move to question me.

He was there because the waitresses had presents for his wife on the occasion of the recent birth of their first child.

I was curious about the tight relationship that existed at that time between Malcolm and Muhammad Ali. First off, I felt impressed by how, unlike so many other famous people who you never get close to, Malcolm was so approachable. Then I was further surprised by how engaging he was, how he made you feel like you were somebody special.

Our dialogue amounted to nothing more than a handshake and a hand-to-heart hug, plus polite "good to meet you" stuff. But I could feel the same kind of vibe that Ali must have felt: that Malcolm X was a man of the people.

Indeed, he provided leadership with his words, and showed character with his actions. But he wasn't addressing the white population. Instead, Malcolm's intent was to induce his Black

Muslim brothers and sisters to accept the thousands of white Muslims he had encountered. This was a challenge to the Black Muslim hierarchy, and the courage he showed meant a great deal even to those Black folks who weren't Muslims. But with this inclusive view, Malcolm effectively signed his own death warrant.

Early in my tenure with the Pistons, I learned how one of the major advances in the improvement of African American lives was the advent of credit unions. My awareness of this began in Detroit, where so many Blacks worked in the auto industry. With the almost universal proliferation of credit cards and, more importantly, credit itself (which had been mostly unavailable to African Americans previously), brothers and sisters could now buy cars, appliances, and even homes.

A new feeling of freedom was everywhere in the late 1960s. Young white people started wearing tie-dyed shirts, beads, dashikis, platform shoes, long hair, even Afros, and began to be identified by the media as "Hippies." All of these innovations were part of an expanding manifestation of the new freedom to express one's individual choice in so many ways—including smoking marijuana.

For me, the political system in the late sixties became more attractive because some important African American politicians had come on the scene who had never before held national office or had a national platform but who now began to run for office—namely, Jesse Jackson, Adam Clayton Powell, Edward Brooke, and Shirley Chisholm—with dozens more to come after them. This realization led me to work on off-days for Hubert Humphrey's presidential campaign in 1968.

Along with Joey Bishop, Billy Cunningham, Willie Wood, Chet Walker, and Earnest Evans (better known as "Chubby Checker"), I was part of the vice president's entourage whenever he made appearances in Philly, Washington, DC, and Baltimore. It was an honor to connect with him. Of course, Senator (and Vice President) Hubert Humphrey got caught in the line of anti–Vietnam War fire after LBJ decided not to seek reelection and Humphrey ran in his place. This turned out to be an unfortunate series of events. I found HH to be a good man, a genuine humanitarian, as well as being a very deliberate thinker.

After MLK was gunned down, I was Mrs. Coretta Scott King's bodyguard when she came to Baltimore. To be in her presence was inspirational, although at some point I realized that my ability to protect her was limited, since I was unarmed.

CHAPTER TEN

THE BROTHERS CHANGE THE GAMES AND THEIR NAMES

In 1968, Lew Alcindor converted to Sunni Islam and privately changed his "slave name" to Kareem Abdul-Jabbar. (He made this official in 1971.) He then boycotted the 1968 Olympic Games to protest the unequal treatment of African Americans in the USA.

According to the newspapers and the call-in sports-talk radio shows, he instantly became unpopular among many white fans and sportswriters. With Milwaukee, Kareem underwent continuous harassment, and he was getting death threats, which caused delays for the teams at airports when the team was on the road. Wherever the Bucks played, the NBA had to provide extra security for Kareem.

A major reason so many white people turned against him was that they didn't really understand the difference between a Black Muslim and a Black Panther. Even though Kareem was associated with a more peaceful branch of the Black Muslim group, many whites imagined him wearing a black beret, dressed in black clothes, and brandishing an automatic weapon. And they were scared to death.

Conversely, African Americans viewed Kareem as a hero. Since he knew what had happened to Ali when he changed his name, it took a great deal of courage for Kareem to be so out-front in making the change.

Kareem's bravery led a parade of other Black athletes to publicly assume new names and identities. Walt Hazzard became Mahdi Abdul-Rahman. Keith Wilkes became Jamaal Wilkes. Chris Jackson was now Mahmoud Abdul-Rauf. Don Smith was Zaid Abdul-Aziz. And Brian Williams honored his Native American heritage by becoming Bison Dele.

Another racial milestone occurred when Bill Russell became the Celtics' player-coach in 1968. The retiring Red Auerbach had this explanation: "With me out of the picture, who else but Bill Russell could coach Bill Russell?" The result was that Russ became the first African American coach in the history of the NBA. That's when he demonstrated his basketball intelligence by having a heart-to-heart talk with his best player (himself!) and subsequently winning another championship.

Just another note about how good a player Russ was: Too many fans and media who never saw him play believe that he'd never be able to even make a current NBA roster. They simply have no idea of his quickness (within a small area), speed (from end-to-end), athleticism, heart, and awareness. These are things that can't be quantified.

He'd certainly have no trouble preventing a seven-footer from launching a 3-pointer, and then flashing back into the lane to protect the hoop. In fact, the only player since Russ who had the same capability in this respect was Ben Wallace.

In addition, Russell's timing was so exquisite that he could wait until an opponent released his shot before leaping to block it. This meant that no amount of fakes could get Russ to leave his feet prematurely. Plus, instead of the current mucho-macho tendency to ferociously send a blocked shot into the stands, Russ would tap the ball to an area where he knew a teammate was positioned, thus initiating Boston's devastating fast break.

Famously, before every NBA game Russ ever played, he vomited. This manifestation of his nervousness was evidence of his attitude that every game was an ultimate challenge.

As far as physical ability is concerned, Russ was a highly evolved being who was way ahead of the hit parade. The same can be said of Wilt.

Also contrary to popular belief, Russ was not arrogant or antisocial. He was actually very shy and became even more withdrawn whenever everybody stopped talking and stared at him when he entered a room.

Players who are 6′9″ and taller were usually either power forwards or centers, while (with the notable exception of guys like Paul Silas and Bill Bridges), shorter players were most often "small forwards." So there was a sense of camaraderie among us bigs. And, like Russ, we're generally very self-conscious and introverted in crowds of civilians, but we eventually learn how to play the "happy to see you" game. In fact, the only big guy I can recall who is naturally the extroverted life of the party is Shaq. His attitude is: *"The night doesn't begin until I arrive. Here I am so let's get it ON!"*

In the late 1950s, the Rochester Royals played an up-tempo but highly disciplined game. Bobby Wanzer and Bob Davies were effective runners in the backcourt, but the difference was Maurice Stokes (1955–57), a 6′7″, 232-pounder from St. Francis

(PA)—a mostly white college. Stokes was the first forward who could play end-to-end.

For sure, many African American athletes would later be drafted, mainly because, as the racial awareness of the basketball community expanded, more Blacks were named to All-Conference and/or All-American teams. In 1958, Guy Rodgers (Temple) was the first of these, having been drafted by Philadelphia. Later, primary examples would be Cazzie Russell (Michigan), Walt Bellamy (Indiana), and Jim "Bad News" Barnes (Texas Western).

It soon became gospel among NBA scouts that African Americans were extremely athletic. As a result, NBA teams widened their search for outstanding Black undergraduates. This led to an increasing tendency during the 1960s to begin drafting players from HBCU, thus drastically changing the game.

During that time, white players like Jerry Lucas and John Havlicek had great fundamental skills as a result of their being coached as youngsters in CYO, YMCA, and Boys' Clubs leagues and the like. Meanwhile, most Black kids were self-taught, developing their games in schoolyards and playgrounds, and not learning fundamentals until high school. That's why their individualistic, one-on-one moves were more highly developed than those of their white peers.

As a result, the influx of HBCU players made NBA action much more exciting, which led to higher TV ratings and more profits for the league's moguls.

The most impactful of these early draftees were Earl Monroe (Winston-Salem); Mike Davis (Virginia Union); Ed Manning (Jackson State); Willis Reed (Grambling); Woody Sauldsberry (Texas Southern); Earl Lloyd (West Virginia State); Sam Jones (North Carolina Central); Bobby Dandridge (Norfolk State);

Bob Love (Southern); Zelmo Beaty (Prairie View A&M); Elmore Smith and Travis "Machine Gun" Grant (Kentucky State); plus Dick Barnett, Ben Warley, and John Barnhill (all from Tennessee State).

Credit for discovering many of these players goes to Earl Lloyd when he was Detroit's chief scout, and to Red Auerbach and Red Holzman, as well as to Marty Blake.

More recently, it's a common occurrence for players to be drafted from HBCU schools:

From Norfolk State came Kyle O'Quinn. Tennessee State produced Robert Covington, Leonard "Truck" Robinson, and Anthony Mason. Ricky Mahorn from Hampton Institute. Charles Oakley and Ben Wallace (who was undrafted) played at Virginia Union, and many more.

In truth, it was really the NBA, rather than Major League Baseball, that opened their rosters sooner, and wider, to all African American players.

Aside from the difference in the floor game, the appearance of these superathletes was a primary reason why TV ratings went up and, accordingly, so did the NBA's revenue.

Also, as the NBA literally became more colorful, the new players began to adopt colorful nicknames. It should be noted that very few white players had nicknames. A few notable exceptions were Bob Pettit, who was called "Big Blue" because he always wore a battered blue overcoat. Adolph Schayes was a.k.a. "Dolly" as opposed to linking his first name with you know who. Dick McGuire was "Tricky Dick," Harry Gallatin was Harry "The Horse," Joe Fulks was "Jumpin' Joe," Pete Maravich was "Pistol Pete," and Bob Cousy was simply "Cooz." All told, not very imaginative brands. Of course Jerry West was "Zeke from Cabin Creek," which is a winner. And Billy Cunningham was "Kang," which was short for "The Kangaroo Kid" because of his hops. But early superstars such as Paul Arizin, George Mikan, Neil Johnston, and so on were never given nicknames.

Reflecting the change in the overall culture, freedom to express oneself became what the modern player aimed to do. Suddenly, the nicknames of African American players became much more inventive. Is Walt Frazier ever called anything but "Clyde"? Earl Monroe is "The Pearl" and also "Black Jesus." Not to mention Joe "Pogo" Caldwell; Chet "The Jet" Walker; Dave "Bingo" Bing; Nate "Tiny" Archibald; Eddie "The Man with the Golden Arm" Miles; Ed "The Razor" Manning; Mike "The Crusher" Davis; Gus "Honeycomb" Johnson; there's "Magic," "The Beard," "The Greek Freak," "The Stifle Tower," "The Brow," "Jimmy Buckets," "Boogie," "Iso Joe," "Chocolate Thunder," and "White Chocolate."

More importantly, the influx of these HBCU players (and several more) was very instrumental in the creation of the American Basketball Association. In October 1967, when the league began, the ball they used was light, slippery, striped, and a dud. By the time I got there, in 1970, the ABA ball had greatly improved and I came to like it better than the NBA ball.

Also, because of the 3-point line (which the NBA did not install until 1979), deadeye shooters like Louie Dampier, Darel Carrier, Rick Mount, and Billy Keller were among the ABA's best players.

The ABA also provided several African American players the same opportunity to be seen by NBA scouts. Certainly, there were some brothers who were good enough to get drafted by NBA teams but, for various reasons, chose to play in the ABA, where they became stars: George Carter and Cincy Powell are the most notable examples. The ABA also gave guys like Larry, Steve, and Jimmy Jones, also Mack Calvin, the time and place to work on their games until they were signed by NBA teams.

Moreover, Jim "Goose" Ligon had starred at Kokomo High School before getting into trouble and winding up in jail. Yet Ligon got another chance to play competitive basketball when he was signed by the ABA's Kentucky Colonels. During my time in the ABA, I found Goose to be a good player and a good guy.

Another individual who was incredibly instrumental in shaping the rosters of both the ABA and the NBA was Spencer Haywood. By the time he was seventeen and a junior in Detroit's Pershing High School, Spencer was already one of the best non-NBA players in the country, if not the world. He could simply do everything on both ends of the court and in the spaces between them. In 1968, after one season at Trinidad Junior College—where he averaged 28.2 points and 22.1 rebounds—he became, at nineteen, the youngest member of any US Olympic basketball team. Augmented by the considerable talents of Jo Jo White, Charlie Scott, and Mike Silliman (who became the only West Point graduate to play in the NBA—1970 with the Clippers), Haywood was the undisputed star as the US won the Gold Medal in Mexico City.

Spencer's next stop was the University of Detroit (UD), where his numbers were 32.1 points and 22.1 rebounds. Yet because the NBA had ruled that no college players could be drafted until their freshman class had graduated four years late, Spencer would have to play two more years at UD before becoming eligible for the NBA Draft.

Rather than spend those prime seasons competing against other amateur players, he signed with Denver in the ABA—

where he averaged 30.0 points and 19.5 rebounds to lead the league in both categories. He topped off his ABA career by leading Denver to a championship and being named the league's MVP.

Subsequently, the NBA's Seattle SuperSonics signed Spencer to a contract that the NBA said was invalid. It got to the point where Spencer even suited up for the Sonics and took part in the pregame layup lines. But the NBA had him forcibly removed from the court. I always wondered if a white player would have been accorded that treatment in the same situation.

But Spencer refused to give up. He sued the NBA and, with the financial support of Sam Schulman, the Sonics' owner, the case reached the Supreme Court in 1970. The game-changing ruling was that the NBA had no legal grounds to deprive Spencer of an opportunity to further his career. So in the 1970–71 season he became a full-fledged member of the Sonics in time enough to play in thirty-three games—and averaged 20.6 points and 12.0 rebounds. From Seattle, he went on to play for the Knicks, New Orleans, and the Lakers (where he made a significant contribution to their championship), before finishing with Washington.

For his twelve-year NBA career, his total numbers included 19.2 points, 9.3 rebounds, and four appearances in All-Star games.

But the lasting influence of Spencer's actions paved the way for the NBA initially being forced to draft players who declared "Hardship" status. Eventually this led to the drafting of players even before their frosh class graduated, and also drafting some players straight out of high school. These eventually included Darryl Dawkins, Bill Willoughby, Kevin Garnett, LeBron James, Dwight Howard, Lou Williams, Kobe Bryant, Amar'e Stoudemire, Tracy McGrady, and J.R. Smith.

So, in many ways, Spencer Haywood is, and should be, a hero to many players past, present, and future who enter the NBA "early."

Another player who changed the way the NBA did business was Oscar Robertson. The "Big O" was a complete player who could shoot, score, pass, rebound, and defend. I was always most amazed by his passing; his ability to put the ball *right there,* so the receiver didn't have to load up or reposition the ball. Just catch-and-shoot, as if the ball almost bounced off the shooter's hands. When Guy Rodgers, who was point guard, played with Cincinnati (1967–68), Oscar rarely gave up the ball, but Rodgers ran the offense when O was resting on the bench.

Besides his remarkable playing career, it was Oscar who was the major force behind the creation and acceptance of the NBA players' union. So Oscar gets most of the credit for the astounding increase in players' salaries in the past decade.

I played against Oscar many times in the NBA and was honored to play with him during many summers in several Maurice Stokes games at Kutshers, as well as charity Martin Luther King All-Star games. And to sum up my overall impression of Oscar Robertson—on and off the court he was and still is one of the most graceful and forthright men I've ever known.

CHAPTER ELEVEN

FOREVER DIDN'T LAST LONG

January 16, 1967. I'll never forget the date because that's when I was traded from Detroit to the Baltimore Bullets. Getting dealt from a team and a city where you started and where you built your career for some years (six in my case) is always a complicated situation. But this particular trade was even more complicated than usual.

The original deal had Rudy LaRusso going from the Lakers to Detroit, with Mel Counts going from Baltimore to the Lakers, and me going to Baltimore. But LaRusso simply refused to report to Detroit.

He decided that, since his wife was pregnant, making such a radical move was not an option. Moreover, he had gone to college at Dartmouth in Hanover, NH, where the winters are brutally frigid and snowbound, so he knew how bad winter can be. It's easy to think that Rudy also wanted no part of leaving the beaches and the sunshine to plunge back into long, shivering winter seasons.

The revised trade had Counts and me resettling as before, but LaRusso was suspended by Los Angeles and quickly announced his retirement. In his place, the Lakers sent a number-one draft pick to the Pistons.

It also turned out that because he sat out a season, LaRusso became an unrestricted free agent. The next year, he signed with the San Francisco Warriors, where he continued his excellent career for two more seasons until an injury forced his retirement.

The ten days it took for the whole thing to be worked out were some of the worst days of my life. I was in limbo and very lonely. But I persevered, diligently working out every day at the Fisher YMCA in Detroit. Shooting, running, just trying to stay in shape.

My NBA roots were in Detroit, so I felt I was in terrible straits, but a few nights before I left, Dave Bing and Eddie Miles took me to the 20 Grand club to see Aretha Franklin. I had first met her many years ago at the Pink Poodle when the Pistons were playing an exhibition game in Indianapolis. The club was packed, and after her first set Aretha was looking for somewhere to sit so she could relax until her next set began. It just so happened that the only empty chair was at my table, so that's where she sat down.

This was quite a thrill, because Aretha was universally acknowledged as the Queen of Soul. I mean, she was up there with Billie Holiday, Ella Fitzgerald, Dinah Washington, and Sarah Vaughan in the pantheon of true royalty. Also, having routinely appeared on Johnny Carson's and many of the other late-night shows, Aretha was extremely popular.

Her demeanor was queenly, but Aretha treated me with warmth and respect. She had been born in Tennessee and her family moved to Detroit when she was two. Aretha began singing gospel songs in Detroit's New Bethel Baptist Church. By the time I met her, Aretha's open heart toward the Black community in Detroit was well-known and greatly appreciated . . . she was an authentic person.

We had a long, personable conversation about many topics, including life on the road and the responsibility of giving our all in front of people who paid to see us perform. And we became friends.

Whenever Aretha happened to be performing in a city where the Pistons were playing, I made sure to go see her. Even in the off-season, wherever the Queen was, I went and saw her. One time when we were both in Philly, she introduced me to Ted White, her husband. They lived in Detroit at the time, and Teddy was a big Pistons fan.

Fast forward to that unforgettable day in January 1967. My profound sadness at leaving the Motor City and so many friends was instantly changed when Aretha said this from the stage: "My friend, Ray Scott, is here, and I'd like to dedicate this song to him."

Then, as she sang "You're Gonna Hear from Me," I was so touched, appreciation welling up within me, that you could've popped me open with a pin.

When I got to Baltimore, the Bullets were in the process of breaking up the team and starting from scratch. This was a strategy that would soon prove extremely successful.

Meanwhile, my new teammates included:

Leroy Ellis, who at 6'11" could both run and block shots.

Kevin "Murph" Loughery, a deadly shooter, who was also Bronx-tough.

Johnny "Space" Egan, was a hell of a player, whose nickname came because of his ability to elevate, what we called his hops.

Gus Johnson, who was inducted into the Hall of Fame in 2010, but just may be the most underrated player honored there.

The thirty-four-year-old Johnny Green, who still had significant hops when he retired five years later.

And a reunion with John Barnhill, a smaller "rabbit" who could run and defend.

They were all good guys.

The coach was Gene Shue, who was a former Detroit teammate of mine. Where many NBA coaches look to fit players into their habitual systems, Gene coached to the individual strengths of his players. He was a good coach.

At first I was somewhat apprehensive about living and working in what was widely known to be a Southern city. Indeed, I still retained a really bad memory of the first time I had been there.

That was in 1958 when I was playing with Allentown in the Eastern League and we had a road game with the Baltimore Bullets. We went to a restaurant called the White Castle (not the franchised hamburger joint of the same name) for our pregame meal. The white guys on the team sat at the counter—they were Brendan McCann, Jerry Paulson, Tom Hart, Kurt Engelbert, and Art Spoelstra. Meanwhile, Sonny Hill and I, the only African American players, sat at a table. After a while, my white teammates came over to say that the restaurant told them that they didn't serve Black people. Spoelstra, from Western Kentucky, took the lead, insisting that we all walk out. We were all agreeable, but we subsequently couldn't find another place to eat that would serve all of us. So we got to the arena prepared to play without our normal pregame meal. But the owner of the Jets, John Kimock, went out and brought back some food, which we ate even as we were getting into our uniforms.

I don't remember who won the game, but I like to think that we did.

When I first arrived in Baltimore after the 1967 trade, I was put up in the swanky Lord Baltimore Hotel. From a window in my room, I could see that same White Castle restaurant. I could now see Black folks entering and leaving the place, but I was never going to be one of them.

Despite my uneasiness, I was surprised to discover that there were some African Americans employed throughout the organization. Credit Abe Pollin, the primary owner of the team, for dealing with racism in a positive, meaningful way.

Once Earl Monroe joined the team for the 1966–67 season, our home attendance greatly increased. Plus, the fans at the games were 100 percent Bullets' partisans, who paid no attention to whether we were Black or white.

I eventually rented an apartment on the outskirts of Baltimore and greatly enjoyed my time there. There was always good jazz somewhere in the city—Les McCann, Charles Mingus, the Modern Jazz Quartet, and Roberta Flack. And even Rufus Harley, who played jazz on bagpipes. Plus, DC clubs were a short trip away.

Another reason why I was so happy to join the Bullets was their eagerness to raise my salary. During my tenure in Baltimore, the owners of the team, Abe Pollin, Earl Foreman, and Arnie Hoeft, generously increased my pay from the teens, where it had been previously, to a hefty $40,000 per season. I was twenty-seven, and thus seemed to me like all the money in the world.

I was also surprised by the social situation among my teammates, because, Black and white, we all hung out together. In fact, I spent a lot of time with Jack Marin, who was devoted to the teachings of Ayn Rand. Despite our differences, we debated with great vigor and always enjoyed each other's company.

I was also able to socialize frequently with some of the legendary Baltimore icons who all lived in the city and not in the suburbs. From the Orioles, Frank and Brooks Robinson, and Boog Powell. From the Colts, Johnny Unitas and John Mackey.

During my three and a half years in Baltimore, the city was changing. For many, many years Baltimore had been known as Charm City and was recognized to be closely affiliated with the Jim Crow culture of the South. The change was mostly due to the students at the seventeen colleges in the immediate area. Among these schools were Loyola, University of Maryland, Towson, Bowie State, and Morgan State. Gradually the students took over downtown, and the city became much more integrated. There were (and still are) fair-housing and school-integration issues, yet everything was mostly peaceful and "groovy." Until, that is, the assassination of Dr. Martin Luther King.

The mayor was Thomas D'Alesandro III, who was known to everybody as "Young Tommy." I encountered him in political situations, along with his sister, Nancy D'Alesandro Pelosi. The mayor did all he could to bring Baltimore into the twentieth century.

The city has never recovered from MLK's tragic death and the drug culture that became dominant afterward. The municipal budget had been cut to the point where the police force was unable to modernize and so could not inhibit the surge of available drugs and drug-related crimes. For a realistic representation of what Baltimore eventually became, see the HBO televisons series *The Wire*.

Meanwhile, the rebuilding of the Bullets took off when Earl Monroe was drafted during my second year in Baltimore. He was simply amazing. One of those players who made even NBA veterans say, "I never saw that kind of move before." As a rookie, Earl immediately demonstrated that he was at the level of the best guards in the league—Dave Bing (who had led the NBA in scoring), Jerry West, Walt Frazier, and Oscar Robertson. Moreover, Earl was also a defensive stalwart, because he could read offenses and effectively play for steals.

Then, a year later (1968), Wes Unseld was drafted—a guy who seemed to grab every rebound and eventually became the only player other than Wilt who was both the MVP and the Rookie of the Year. So we were ready to challenge the Knicks for supremacy in the Eastern Conference. Which we did, only to lose to them twice in the conference finals.

As for me, with Earl, Loughery, Jack Marin, Gus Johnson, and Wes Unseld on the floor, I got fewer and fewer shots from season-to-season. That's why my points per game steadily decreased from 19.0 to 16.4 to 11.8, then to 8.9. Even so, through it all, my primary job was to rebound. Out of all my NBA stats, the ones I'm proudest of were having two 1,000-rebound seasons (1963–64 in Detroit and 1967–68 in Baltimore). These place me sixty-second in the NBA's 1,000-rebound club. I may be way down, but I'm still on the list. Another number that I cherish is having averaged 10.5 rebounds throughout my NBA career.

In addition to my rebounding, there were seasons when my point averages were as high as 17.6 (1963–64), 17.9 (1965–66), and topped out at 19.0 during my half season in 1968 with Baltimore. Which sometimes led me to wonder why I was never named to an All-Star team. Especially since some players with lower stats did make the grade. There were guys like Bailey Howell, Dave DeBusschere, Terry Dischinger, Tom Meschery, and Rudy LaRusso, who were ahead of me. All white guys.

Don't get me wrong. These guys were all great players, who had major college pedigrees.

And, hey. I have absolutely no complaints. What is, is, and what was, was.

In any event, throughout my stay in Baltimore, several teams presented us with challenges. The best of these was the Boston Celtics, led by Bill Russell, and ably abetted by Tom Sanders, John Havlicek, also Sam Jones and K.C. Jones. However, some of our most hard-fought, competitive, and popular contests (especially in the playoffs) were played against the New York Knicks. Even though their offense was as predictable and well-choreographed as a Broadway musical, even though we knew what they wanted to do, we simply couldn't stop them. "Hit the open man" was Red Holzman's mantra, without ever specifying who that man would or should be—and they always did. Even worse, they never seemed to miss their open shots.

That's Clyde and Barnett in the backcourt, the former couldn't be stopped when he got the ball fifteen feet from the hoop, the latter subjugated his offense and concentrated on defense—even so, his Fall Back Baby jumpshot could still score when he had to.

Plus, since Reed, Bradley, Cazzie, and DeBusschere were such good outside shooters, they were able to position Frazier down in the low post to take advantage of certain deficient defenders. And then there was Willis, who routinely owned the pivot—country-strong, fearless, and quick-footed.

They were just as tough on defense. Clyde was much stronger and quicker than he appeared to be. He could get in the face of an opposing point guard and literally take him out of the game. Nobody defended Jerry West nearly as well as Frazier did.

Basically, their defense was set up to produce steals, and their modus operandi was to force the ball handler to reverse direction. Reed's massive show on high screens was one way they accomplished this. Whoops! The guy would see Reed's big body waiting for him and make a U-turn—and there was Frazier, Barnett, Dean Meminger, or (later) Monroe just waiting to snipe the ball away.

Also, the Knicks didn't look to switch when confronted with screens. Instead, they simply fought their way through the obstacles.

They were almost one of the NBA's greatest teams. I have nothing but tremendous admiration for them.

After my NBA days were over, in addition to the Celtics and the Knicks, I always enjoyed watching the Seattle SuperSonics. With "Downtown" Freddie Brown, Donald "Slick" Watts, Dennis Johnson, Kermit Washington, Gus Williams, John Johnson, Paul Silas, Lonnie Shelton, as well as Jack Sikma with his face-up moves, the Sonics played beautiful, team-oriented basketball.

Yet, even though Seattle beat the supremely talented Washington Bullets (with Elvin Hayes, Wes Unseld, Bob Dandridge, Kevin Grevey and a solid bench) for the championship in 1979, the Sonics never got the respect they deserved. The reason being that on the media-heavy East Coast their games were played at 10:00 p.m. and were therefore underexposed.

By the 1968–69 season, my playing time was diminished. That's because Earl Monroe (25.8), Kevin Loughery (22.6), Jack Marin (15.9), Wes Unseld (13.8), and Gus Johnson (17.9) were doing more and more of the scoring. I actually started the 1968–69 season on the bench, but took Johnson's place when he was injured, and ended up averaging 11.8—the lowest point production I'd ever had until my 8.9 average in the following season. Even worse, I was used sparingly in 1969–70, and only averaged 4 points in the playoffs.

My lack of minutes made it clear to me that I was done in Baltimore.

That's why, in the middle of the season, I asked Shue to be traded. He refused, saying, "I may need you." However, at the end of the season, I was made available to be picked by one of the NBA's new teams—the Portland Trail Blazers and the Buffalo Braves.

Subsequently, I became the Braves' very first pick in the expansion draft. Other players who wound up in Buffalo included Bob Kauffman, Don May, Dick Garrett, John Hummer, Herm Gilliam, Emmette Bryant, Bill Hosket, Walt Hazzard, Nate Bowman, and Mike Silliman. So the Braves looked to be a halfway decent team.

Okay. So I went up to Buffalo, where I met with the general manager, Eddie Donovan, and the team president, Carl Scheer.

I was thirty-two at the time and beginning to suffer from what was called Jumper's Knee. This was primarily caused by playing so much on outdoor courts, either on cement or on asphalt. Besides quickly wearing out sneakers, the solid, abrasive surfaces increased the shock to the legs of players who had better than average hops.

However, even then, and with nine NBA seasons behind me, I still had plenty of gas left in my tank. So I was open to becoming an original member of the Braves.

My aim during the meeting was to find out what was the team's game plan. How did they feel their new players would fit together? Were more trades in the offing? What would my salary be?

However, Scheer was very rude. He treated me like I was just a pain in the ass. He said it was "premature" to talk about their game plan, and also "premature" to discuss salary.

Then I was summarily dismissed!

So I went home, thinking I was done with the NBA.

Looking back at my nine-year NBA playing career and traveling all around the country, I see that I gained a new perspective on the league, on the players, on myself, and on America. For the most part, my experience only reinforced some of my old viewpoints.

I'd always been aware of the so-called NBA Halo, and I certainly enjoyed the status and the partying. But I was never a true believer, so I didn't buy into all that celebrity stuff. Beneath the glitter and hero-worshipping, NBA players were people.

Off the court, there's a basic insecurity that Black guys my size have. We can't hide, and everybody turns to stare when we walk down the street or enter a room where there are people we don't know. We don't blend in easily, and we're aware that some of these strangers will resent us.

Members of a dominant race or class of people don't really have to care what others say about them. A race or class of people that are in the minority don't have that luxury. So most African American athletes can instinctively tell if somebody really likes us, or only likes what we represent or what we can do. For many of us, and especially for me, we just want people to like us for who we really are.

There are fifty-four countries on the continent of Africa, but most of the 235 million whites in America think of Africa as if it were a single country. So they look at the 47 million American Blacks as being all the same and only judge us by the color of our skin. Meanwhile, the majority of whites are aware of their own cultural differences. Europeans are different from Irish, Greeks are different from Italians or Albanians or Armenians or Turks. Whatever. Yet there are significant cultural differences, and in some cases long histories of conflict, among most of the African countries and tribes, no different from the kinds of wars or conflicts that existed between, say, the French and the English. In addition, many tribes were divided and pitted against one another by European colonization. The Igbos. The Hausa. My people came from Nigeria, but in America I am always referred to as a Black man or an African American.

Indeed, the culture of most African tribes goes back thousands of years. Meanwhile, the culture of Blacks in America goes back only a few hundred years. As a result, we've had to create our own culture, which, in many ways, has been co-opted by whites.

Whites tend to believe that their culture is superior to the African American culture. For the most part, in any country the dominant race or class of people claims to have all the answers. We don't accept many of those answers, but we have to live with them.

PART THREE

CHAPTER TWELVE

THAT'S WHAT I LIKE ABOUT THE SOUTH

A friend advised me to talk to Earl Foreman, who owned the Virginia Squires in the ABA. This franchise was originally owned by Pat Boone and played its inaugural season in Oakland. Rick Barry was the star of the franchise and was also the player the ABA owners thought could lead the league into financial success. But his presence failed to generate the expected attention and revenue in Oakland, and since Boone was running out of money, he sold the team to Mr. Foreman, who moved it to Washington, DC. However, since the Capital Center, home to the Baltimore Bullets, was less than an hour's drive away from DC, Mr. Foreman's new purchase had a small fan base. Why watch the Washington Caps when you could drive a short distance to see Earl Monroe, Gus Johnson, Wes Unseld, and company? Sure, Rick Barry was always worth seeing, but what about Gary Bradds, Hal Jeter, Rick Warren, Henry Logan, and Frank Card? All very good players, but lacking the pizzazz of the NBA players.

When Mr. Foreman announced that the next reincarnation of the franchise would be in Virginia, Barry wanted out. Rick famously said that he didn't want to raise his kids in the South and hear them say "y'all."

I had signed with the Bullets on my own because, back in those days, most NBA organizations refused to deal with agents. I thought I had signed a guaranteed three-year contract worth $30K-$35K-$40K, but when a Squires' lawyer looked at the contract, he told me that it was actually three one-year deals. I was in the second year, which meant that Buffalo could have cut me at any time. Knowing this, I followed in the footsteps of Rick Barry and Zelmo Beaty by going to court and winning my case, which allowed me to play in the ABA.

When I first talked to Mr. Foreman, he said he was very interested in having me join his team. Then, when I met Mr. Foreman in DC, he quickly offered me a three-year guaranteed contract calling for $50,000 (which is the present-day equivalent of $335,662) for each of two years as a player, then $25,000 for working in the front office. Plus, I was handed $1,000 ($6,713 today) in cash as a signing bonus.

Okay! Not only did I get a long-term secure contract, the Squires also paid for my moving expenses from Baltimore to Norfolk.

The Squires played their home games in four locations: Richmond, Norfolk, Roanoke, and Hampton Road. The coach was Al Bianchi, and my new teammates included Neil Johnson, Roland "Fatty" Taylor, Doug Moe, Jim "Jumbo" Eakins, Larry Brown, George Irvine, George Carter, Mike Maloy, and Charlie Scott, who was the league's leading scorer. Also my buddy, Mike "Birdman" Barrett. A really good group of guys and an exceptional team.

Neil and I were the NBA veterans on the team, and the young guys depended on us to be solid and keep them grounded.

At the time, only a few guys in the early ABA were making NBA money. We were just a bunch of cats playing basketball and enjoying what we were doing.

In any event, the Squires were warmly embraced by the populace in the Tidewater area. Overall, the time I spent with the Squires was the happiest two years in my basketball life. Another reason was the big-time entertainment in the Norfolk Scope and the Hampton Coliseum, where I saw the Rolling Stones, the Temptations, and Glen Campbell.

I loved New York City, so during the off-season I would fly there from Norfolk with some friends and spend a few days seeing Broadway shows like *Hair* and *Blues for Mister Charlie*. We'd also go to clubs to hear jazz, and see entertainers that I remembered from the Borscht Belt, especially Henny Youngman and Rodney Dangerfield.

Back on the court, the Squires ran, ran, then kept on running, with Fatty Taylor setting the pace. I backed up Eakins at the center spot, and we could still run when I was in the game but were also capable of playing efficient half-court offense. Either way, I got a lot of ball time (14.3 points plus 8.0 rebounds per game). I could face-up the bigger opponents and take everybody else into the pivot. Also, because of the 3-point line and the terrific shooters we had, I couldn't be doubled so I always worked one-on-one. And if the ball was coming in, it was not going out!

If Charlie Scott hadn't been injured, I'm convinced we would have won the championship.

There were two major developments in my second season. My knees began to act up so that I could only play in fifty-five games while averaging 7.6 points and 4.6 rebounds. At that point I knew that my eleven-year active career was over, even though I averaged 12.0 points in the playoffs . . .

The second development was the addition of Julius Erving. Coming out of the University of Massachusetts, Julius had had some exposure playing in the National Invitation Tournament (NIT), but with mixed results. In 1970, UMass lost a competitive first-round game to Marquette (62–55) in which Erving scored 21. A year later, North Carolina clobbered them (90–49) in another first-round loss. In this game, Erving produced only 13 points and 9 rebounds, the only contest in his UMass career in which he didn't put up a double-double.

But Earl Foreman had the foresight to draft Erving, and once he joined the Squires, Doc soon proved to be a truly transcendent player. He simply excelled in every aspect of the game. Offense, defense, rebounding, passing, shooting, doing whatever we needed to win.

Unfortunately, Charlie Scott was off to Phoenix after the last game of the regular season. Julius picked up the slack in the playoffs, averaging 40 points, 20 rebounds, and 10 assists as we beat the Floridians. Then we lost to the New York Nets in the conference finals.

When Julius finally arrived in the NBA, the dreaded Jumper's Knee greatly hindered his play. So, as great as he still was, NBA watchers never saw him at his best.

More importantly, Julius Erving was an even better person than he was a player.

In retrospect, and even though the ABA only lasted ten years, the league still had a profound effect on the evolution of the NBA. That's simply because it brought professional basketball to parts of the country that had never experienced that kind of competition. Add the red-white-and-blue ball and the 3-point shot, and the ABA created fans of pro ball in places like

Memphis, St. Louis, Salt Lake City, Pittsburgh, Denver, San Antonio, Miami, Charlotte, and Louisville.

There was no national TV, so players like Bob Netolicky, Rick Mount, Ron Boone, and dozens of others rarely played before more than two thousand fans. And that's who they played their hearts out for, which was why there was more of a fans-players connection in the ABA than there was in the NBA.

My total numbers attest to my having been a useful professional player. Yet, like virtually all such players, there were some holes in my game. My best attributes were shooting, handling, jumping, and rebounding, but I was never as strong as I could/ should have been. I came into the NBA weighing 220, bulked up to 238, then slimmed down to 228, a weight that prevented me from getting routinely bullied by bigger, stronger opponents.

I also lacked the quickness to play deny defense, a quality that guys like Jack Marin and Wayne Hightower had mastered. This was a problem because once the likes of Rick Barry got the ball, most defenders became not-so-innocent bystanders. Sometimes I could shoot the gap and make a steal, but I mostly tried to play one-on-one defense before my opponent got the ball. Satch Sanders excelled at this—knowing your man's favorite spot and bumping him off of it.

Big players who were deadly shots gave me the most trouble—guys like Barry Clemens and Fred Hetzel. Where Gus Johnson could block their shots, it was all I could do to keep a body on them.

Yet my more serious flaw was being a right-handed player in a right-handed league. I could dribble left and pull for a jumper, and also dribble left to the hoop. But once I got to the basket, I had to improvise some kind of finish with my right hand.

Overall, I can say that in addition to whatever skills and talent I was blessed with, I was not deficient in hustling, studying my opponents, and being a team-oriented player. As I've mentioned previously, the difference was coaching.

It started in high school with Doug Connally, who helped me understand that I had potential. Then, during my abbreviated college career, and later in the NBA, I was fortunate to have some excellent coaches: Dick McGuire, Earl Lloyd, Gene Shue, and Al Bianchi—all of whom were instrumental in enabling me to fulfill my potential. During that same period, however, there were plenty of other African American players who were not fortunate enough to have the same opportunities.

With my playing career over, Mr. Foreman said I could have any position in the organization except coach and his job. I wound up wearing a suit and tie, traveling around the Tidewater area, talking to various groups, and selling season tickets. I was answerable only to Mr. Foreman, and I loved what I was doing. I worked through lunch from 9 to 3 and was on the beach by 4:00. I did this from April and into August, until I got a call from Earl Lloyd, who was now the head coach of the Pistons.

"Ray," he said. I need you to come help me coach these guys."

I went to Mr. Foreman and told him that I simply couldn't turn Earl down, and he was totally agreeable.

(By the way, I refer to *Mr.* Foreman, *Mr.* Coil, and *Mr.* Zollner as a sign of respect for their support and honesty.)

So, goodbye to wonderful Virginia and the ABA. And hello again to Detroit.

CHAPTER THIRTEEN

DETROIT REDUX WITH A FEW MAJOR SURPRISES

When I arrived in Detroit in September 1972, the Pistons matched the $25,000 I was due in my third year with the Squires. I hadn't squandered my previous earnings, so I was fine with that offer.

My first job was to work what was called an "open" camp, which featured free agents and rookies. While I was on the court, I noticed that some of the Pistons' veterans were standing around and watching. Most notably Bob Lanier, Dave Bing, and Curtis Rowe. I'd never played against these guys and I realized that I was starstruck. I felt like I was more of a fan than a coach.

Once "closed" camp was under way, I ran the drills, officiated some scrimmages, and got acquainted with the players I didn't know. I also worked with Rowe to improve his offense—mostly his rhythm and his release. I also played him one-on-one and greatly appreciated his desire to learn.

Once the games began, Earl was what I call an "actionable coach," passionately involved in every play, every substitution, and every call. My main task was to sit quietly and take rather esoteric stats, such as counting defensive denials, showings on screens, effective passes into Lanier at the low post.

Then we were in Portland with a record of 2–5, I was in Earl's room and he had not even unpacked when he got a call from Mr. Coil, the Pistons' general manager, who asked us to come see him. After brief pleasantries when we arrived in his suite, Mr. Coil said he had talked to the owner of the team, Fred Zollner, and they had agreed to make a change. "Earl, you're out. That's what Mr. Zollner wants."

Earl just said, "Okay."

I've discovered that rich people, white and Black, very rarely give reasons why they make decisions like this. I mean, Earl was fired as if he was a chauffeur. But then Mr. Coil turned to me, saying, "And, Ray, you're in."

"What?!"

And I hesitated, until Earl looked at me and said, "Ray, you gotta take this."

After Mr. Coil left, Earl and I spent the rest of the night talking. I was more concerned with how he was feeling than I was about becoming a head coach in the NBA. But he gave me advice, scouting reports on every player on the team, and the defense-oriented game plan that we had both worked up.

On the road, Earl enforced a strict curfew, but after word got around that he was fired, all of the players immediately left the hotel. Leaving me as their coach not knowing where any of them were!

Since early-morning shootarounds were not yet standard in the NBA, my first meeting with my team was in the locker room before the game the next night.

This initial face-off was pressure driven, but I channeled the lessons and examples provided by Earl Lloyd, Al Bianchi, and

Gene Shue. For sure I was nervous, yet I had studied Portland's roster, and came up with a game plan. My new players were totally compliant, one reason being that they wanted to prove that Earl's having been fired was not their fault. This is usually the case in such situations.

Another reason why all went so well was the veteran leadership of Dave Bing. He was the model of respect and goodwill, and he set the tone for his teammates.

During the game, I sometimes consulted the notes I had written, focused on the matchups and on who was showing signs of fatigue, and was able to maintain my concentration throughout. Not only did I not feel overwhelmed, I felt that I was in charge of the players.

The happy result was an exciting win!

Next up was a game in Oakland versus the Warriors, who were led by Rick Barry, Nate Thurmond, and Cazzie Russell. Previously, Bing had been chosen to take the last-second win-or-lose shot. However, I explained to him that if the same situation arose, I would put the ball in Lanier's hands. That's because a talented big man like Lanier had to be the bulwark of our team. Bing readily agreed.

Okay. So Lanier got the ball, made a really good move against Thurmond, missed the shot, but was clearly fouled. No call was made, and I didn't really expect one because NBA refs habitually refuse to have a game decided at a last-second free throw. So we lost another close game.

The Lakers were the third game I coached. They had Wilt, Jerry West, Gail Goodrich, and Flynn Robinson and were the defending champs. This game and its aftermath became a key factor in how the rest of the season unfolded.

Wilt opened the game with four straight dunks, so we were behind 8–0 at the get-go. Our deficit increased to 15 at the half, but on the way to the locker room, I saw Lanier laughing and joking with his buddy Flynn.

The room was quiet when I took Lanier to task. "Why did you do that, Bob? You're supposed to be one of the leaders of this team."

I started Jim Davis in his spot to start the second half, and kept Lanier on the bench for the duration. Late in the third quarter we narrowed the gap to 4 points, but the Lakers stepped on the gas and narrowly won the game.

In the postgame locker room, Lanier said this to me: "I can't play for you." Then he went up to Mr. Coil and repeated his statement. After I dealt with the media, I approached Mr. Coil and said, "This guy can't play for me."

Later, Mr. Coil summoned Lanier and me to meet him in the hotel suite. "Bob," he said, "I'm not going to trade you." Then he turned to me. "Ray, I'm not going to fire you. . . . You two have to settle this by yourselves."

This demonstrated to both Bob and me that I had the backing of the organization, and was at least temporarily in the command seat. The key word here is "temporarily." Even so, Bob was amenable to my game plan.

As a result, Bob played his butt off, leading us to a solid win in Seattle. The road trip ended with a loss to the Houston Rockets in San Antonio—a game in which Lanier scored 42.

Back in Detroit, we beat Philadelphia, and afterward, Mr. Zollner said to me, "You're doing a good job, Ray. There's more harmony on the team than there was."

Even though I felt we were a harmonious team when Earl was the coach, this was the only hint I ever received that might have explained why he was fired. Earl and I agreed that the real problem with the team was that we needed to add more talent off the bench.

Perhaps, Mr. Zollner's feeling about our "harmony" might have been due to what he had been told about the discussions the players routinely had in the locker room. The talk centered on their growing awareness of civil rights and the positive influence of Dr. King and Malcolm X. Even though white players were now in the minority, everybody participated. Plus, the players all hung together on the road.

Doc Schockro was our trainer, a position on most teams that included being the coach's confidant. But Doc only kept me advised on injuries and rehab. Still, the players would bust his chops. After getting his ankles taped and shooting the breeze with some of his teammates, Bing turned to Doc and said, "Hey, Doc. Did you get that?"

Yet after one aggravating loss, Doc gave me this critical advice: "After a game like this, do something wholesome for yourself. Go to a movie, learn to socialize, something. If not, you'll just sit by yourself at home or in a hotel, and you'll come to hate your players. That's how too many coaches start to drink."

I had no assistant coach, but because I had played in the league for so long, I had friends at every stop. Abdul-Rahman (a Philly guy) in LA, Bells in Atlanta. Archie Clark in Baltimore. Plus my family in Philly. And in New York, there was always a trip to Birdland and a dozen of us sitting down to dinner either before or after.

Also, as we started winning, more sportswriters began to show up. Being careful of what I said to them, I started socializing with some of these guys. However, there were some sportswriters who treated me like an interloper.

On November 11, we lost a tight game in Boston. That's when the team's general manager, Ed Coil, offered me a contract as an "interim coach" to finish the season with a prorated raise that was almost twice my assistant coach's salary. I told him that being an interim coach meant that the players really didn't have to listen to me since I'd probably be gone after the season. I also told Mr. Coil that I believed I could bring this team to the next level. With that, the proffered contract was amended to include the following two seasons. Now I felt secure.

After Earl was fired, Mr. Coil pulled the trigger and we added John Mengelt and Don Adams, which helped us on both ends of the court. We finished the season at 40–42, and my record was 38–37. Even more promising, we finished out at 21–9 and missed the playoffs by two games.

We still needed one more player—a frontcourt shooter who could relieve Adams and Rowe. I had my eye on the hot-shooting George "Instant Heat" Trapp, and we eventually worked out a trade to get him from Atlanta. The cost was our number-one draft pick, which I considered to be a good deal because it would only be the tenth overall selection. With the addition of Trapp, I was eagerly looking forward to my first full year on the job.

[PREVIOUS PAGE] In my new uniform with the number George Yardley wore.

[RIGHT] Me at age 10.

[BELOW] My 1958 West Philadelphia High School Championship Team.

Could this be the only rebound I ever grabbed against Wilt?

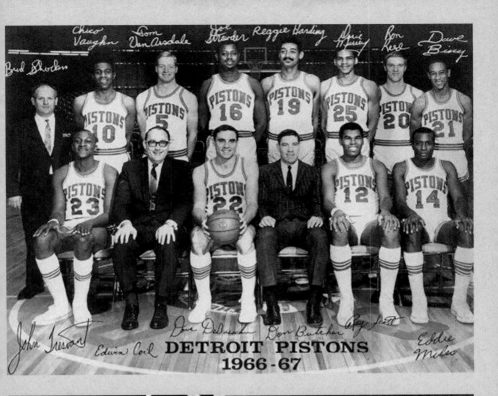

Chico Vaughn • Tom Van Arsdale • Joe Strawder • Reggie Harding • Dave Murray • Ron Reed • Dave Bisey

Bud Shocktn • John Tresvant • Edwin Cork • Dave DeBusschere • Don Butcher • Ray Scott • Eddie Miles

DETROIT PISTONS
1966-67

[FACING PAGE] **Out-rebounding Bob Boozer. Not easy to do.**

[ABOVE] **Dave DeBusschere's first full season as player-coach.**

[LEFT] **A finger-roll over Dave Gambee.**

[RIGHT] **Going one-on-one against Rudy LaRusso, the guy I was traded for.**

RAY SCOTT
forward

BALTIMORE

[ABOVE] A short pop in the paint over Russ Cunningham. Fred Hetzel and Bob Weiss (21) watching.

[TRADING CARD, FACING PAGE, TOP LEFT] The 1968 Eastern Division champs.

[FACING PAGE, TOP RIGHT] Working in the pivot against Al Tucker, with "Hazz" coming in for a steal.

[FACING PAGE, LEFT] A tip-in with Phil Jackson and Willis Reed looking on.

[FACING PAGE, RIGHT] An offensive rebound over Paul Silas. Also not easy to do.

RAY SCOTT
SQUIRES' FORWARD-CENTER

[FACING PAGE, TOP] With the Virginia Squires. Left to right, "Jumbo" Jim Eakins, me, Coach Al Bianchi, Rod Taylor.

[FACING PAGE, LEFT] Intra-squad game, doubling George Carter, a great guy, RIP.

[FACING PAGE, RIGHT] After making a crossover dribble, here's a jumper over Tom "Trooper" Washington.

[ABOVE] My retirement ceremony, flanked by Red Kerr and my proud mom.

[TRADING CARD, LEFT] Happy in Virginia.

[RIGHT] Me and Rod Thorn at an autograph signing with two fans at Hudson's Department Store in Detroit.

Ray Scott—Coach
Director of Player Personnel

[FACING PAGE, TOP LEFT] A bodyguard for Mrs. Coretta King.

[FACING PAGE, TOP RIGHT] The Champ and I.

[FACING PAGE, BOTTOM] A soap box derby for charity.

[ABOVE] A coach at work.

[FACING PAGE, TOP LEFT] Defiance.

[FACING PAGE, LEFT] On the bench with Bob Lanier.

[ABOVE] In-game strategy.

[LEFT] Holding the Red Auerbach Coach of the Year trophy.

[RIGHT] Armed with two of the best.

With Earl Monroe at our 1993 induction into the Philadelphia Sports Hall of Fame.

[BELOW]**With Wilt, two old friends sharing a laugh.**

[LEFT] Mark Andrew with the Best Man at his wedding.

[BELOW, LEFT] With Jack McCloskey, the general manager who put the championship Pistons on the map.

[BELOW, RIGHT] The Black Philadelphia Basketball Hall of Fame.

[ABOVE] **Some Philly-born elite. Hal Lear in front (left to right), Hal Greer, me, Wali Jones, Paul Arizin hidden by Mahdi Abdul-Rahman.**

With my beautiful bride, my inspiration for many things, including the writing of this book.

CHAPTER FOURTEEN

"BENNIE AND THE JETS"

Although it would end in profound disappointment, the 1973–74 season was exhilarating.

The Pistons' games at Cobo Hall were like a big party, and we had a theme song that roused the fans—Elton John's "Bennie and the Jets." An organist, Tyrone Hemphill, played the tune and Dennis Rowland sang the words when the Pistons first came onto the court during our pregame warm-ups, also during time-outs, quarter-breaks, the halftime intermissions, and after the game. The song had the perfect rhythm and rallied the fans, who would respond by clapping their hands in time and singing along. At one point, Elton John's agent came to a game to thank us for making the song such a big part of our game-time entertainment.

Several other professional teams had similar routines. Neil Diamond's "Sweet Caroline" was the theme song of the Boston Red Sox. And before the Philadelphia Flyers played every home playoff game, Kate Smith made a personal appearance to sing "God Bless America." The TV program *Soul Train* originated in Chicago, so the song of the same name became the Bulls' theme.

Moreover, the team had a solid game plan that was based on

playing hard defense and sharing the ball. Credit Bing (18.8 points per game), and Lanier (22.5) for sacrificing shots for passes. Plus, Mengelt and Trapp provided productive scoring off the bench.

On defense, we varied our pressures—picking up at three-quarter court, half-court, and springing strategic double teams. Adams and Chris Ford excelled at team defense, while Curtis Rowe was rock-solid and a lock-down one-on-one defender. We finished allowing only 100.3 points per game, fourth best in the league.

Equally important were Ben Kelso and Bobby Nash, the two guys at the far end of the bench. They practiced hard and never complained about their lack of playing time.

We started off at 12–11, but as we increasingly became patient and more disciplined, we began to be competitive with the league's best teams. Plus, there were several key games that boosted our confidence.

The first of these was in Chicago in the middle of November, when we had possession, a 2-point lead, and five seconds on the game clock. The Bulls' obvious plan was to foul somebody ASAP, right? So, as Bing stood with the ball out of bounds on the sideline, it was no secret that a quick pass had to be made and the receiver would then be fouled. Now, since Bing and Adams were buddies, Dave threw the ball to Don.

"I was thinking that I'd get Don two free throws to add to his numbers."

But Chet Walker anticipated the pass, made the interception, was fouled by Bing, and canned a pair of foul shots to send the game into overtime. The Bulls won when Bob Love hit a 22-footer, a shot that was way out of his range.

We were all hurting in the postgame locker room. Dave was

on the verge of tears as he accepted the blame. "I'm sorry," he said. "This'll never happen again."

And it never did.

That loss brought us together as a team, and from there we won 40 of our next 59 games.

The second impactful game was in Portland on February 5, 1974, where the score was tied with five seconds left to play. We ran a side-out-of-bounds play that we had practiced and that worked to perfection when George Trapp scored the winning bucket. The success of this one play greatly increased the players' confidence in themselves.

Moreover, this was the game that convinced us that we were one of the league's elite teams. And we proved this on a subsequent road trip, where we beat Portland, Seattle, the Lakers, Phoenix, Golden State, and San Diego.

We finished at 52–30, the most wins a Pistons team had ever achieved. However, there were two other 50-win teams in the West—Chicago and Milwaukee—so our first-round opponents in the playoffs were the Bulls.

Chris Ford got into early foul trouble in the opening game and was replaced by Stu Lantz, who almost single-handedly won the game for us. Afterward, I explained to Ford that I was going to start Lantz instead of him. Ford agreed that this was appropriate, even though the change moved him behind Lantz, Bing, Mengelt, and out of the rotation.

It was a measure of how special this team was that a starter was willing to make such a drastic sacrifice.

It was a highly competitive series with the average margin of victory, over the course of six games, being only 6.6 points. For the seventh game, Chicago's backcourt of Jerry Sloan and Norm Van Lier were out with injuries and were replaced by Bob Weiss and Rick Adelman. But with Chet Walker and Bob "Butterbean" Love, they were still formidable. Also, their starting center was Clifford Ray, who had been Tom Boerwinkle's backup. The only reason why Ray started was because Boerwinkle had been injured in the first game of the series. As Boerwinkle's replacement, Ray had played well since then, but only in a supporting role.

In my plan for the seventh game, I was prepared for every dribble: Turn this guy right, that guy left, send the other guy to a help spot. But I made a critical mistake—totally ignoring Ray. Since he rarely shot and had only averaged 8.6 points, many of them on put-backs, I didn't in my wildest imagination think that he could hurt us.

In fact, the game was in Chicago, and we had anticipated the win by packing our bags and getting ready to move on to Milwaukee for the next round.

But hurt us Ray did, scoring 23 and grabbing 19 rebounds. He was hitting hook shots, faking and dropping turn-around jumpers, and making bank shots like he was Wilt. I'd never seen Ray do anything like he was doing. As he played the game of his life, I kept saying to myself, "This can't be true."

We lost 96–94, and our season was prematurely over.

The loss was my fault! No question about it.

To this day, I'm still undone by my shortcoming for that incredibly critical game. It was by far the worst mistake I ever made during my 291-game tenure as Detroit's head coach.

My only consolation is that Clifford is a really good guy and, despite the fact that he ruined that season for us, I still rooted for him during the rest of his career.

Here are some names and numbers that might help explain how and why I felt so thrilled to be honored as the first African

American to be named NBA Coach of the Year (COY) in the aftermath of the Pistons' 52-win 1973–74 season, because nobody who gets that kind of recognition ever succeeds without considerable help from others.

The primary credit for my award, of course, goes to all the players. Willie Norwood (8.0 points averaged in 74 games) and Jim Davis (4.2 points in 78 games) were two wily veterans who acted as unofficial assistant coaches in addition to their solid play. Not only did they help me with game-by-game strategies, they also helped me to recognize situations that were happening during games.

In the preceding twenty-eight years since the establishment of the Basketball Association of America (which merged with the National Basketball League in 1949 to become the NBA), there have been a total of nearly four hundred head coaches employed among all three of these organizations. Of these, before me, only three of these have been Black—Bill Russell, Al Attles, and Earl Lloyd—so it has been my honor to stand on the shoulders of these remarkable men. While Russell and Attles both started out as player-coaches, Lloyd was the first to wear a suit and tie and only be a bench coach.

During that 1973–74 season, Blacks comprised 54 percent of the players who appeared in games. In contrast, only 17.6 percent of the entire coaching corps was African American—me, Russ, and Al Attles. (The lack of racial balance is even more pronounced today. In the 2020–21 season, 73 percent of NBA players were Black as contrasted with a mere 23 percent of all the head coaches who were Black.)

Russ was always like a big brother to me, constantly encouraging me throughout, not only that season, but for my entire coaching career. And Lenny Wilkens, both as a player and later as a coach, was also very helpful in many ways.

Since there were only seventeen teams in the NBA, there was a special collegial relationship among most of the coaches. So, white coaches like Cotton Fitzsimmons and Bill Fitch, plus Fred Schaus, who was the general manager of the Lakers, frequently approached me to share their expertise. Among this fraternity of NBA coaches, there wasn't a hint of racism. Indeed, after games, opposing coaches often had dinner together.

I've been told that the relationship among today's coaches is entirely different, however. Back in the day, very few of us had assistant coaches, whereas today's head coaches have large staffs at their disposal—three, four, and even five assistants, plus others who specialize in weight-training, watching and editing videos, and so on. They're constantly surrounded by their own guys, so a certain isolation is inevitable, and there are very few opportunities to socialize with other head coaches.

I believe that another reason this previous attitude of fraternity among coaches has fractured is that there's simply so much money at stake now. In addition to contractual salaries, literally millions of dollars are gained or lost via an extended list of potential bonuses: so much for making the playoffs, so much for winning each round, so much for winning the championship . . . for winning a certain numer of games . . . for being awarded COY, and so on.

It should also be noted that the next African American after me to be named Coach of the Year was Don Chaney of the Houston Rockets—which didn't happen until 1991. Seventeen years after my award!

Since then, eight brothers have won the same recognition:

Lenny Wilkens with Atlanta in 1994.

Doc Rivers with Orlando in 2000.

Avery Johnson with Dallas in 2006.

Sam Mitchell with Toronto in 2007.

Byron Scott with New Orleans in 2008.

Mike Brown with Cleveland in 2009.

Dwane Casey with Toronto in 2018.

And most recently, Monty Williams with Phoenix in 2021

Hopefully many more African American coaches will be hired sooner rather than later so that many more will succeed the ten of us as NBA Coach of the Year.

CHAPTER FIFTEEN

THE NOT-SO-FORTUNATE FALL

If the 1973–74 season seemed to be a joyful blur, the next season was slow, grueling, and extremely disappointing. And it all started before that 52-win season was over.

Here was the pebble that started the landslide:

The day after we lost that painful seventh game to Chicago, Mr. Zollner summoned Mr. Coil and me for a meeting in a hotel lobby. That's when he told us that he was selling the team for $8.1 million.

I knew that Mr. Zollner had a very long history with the Pistons. What was then called "the Fort Wayne Zollner Pistons" was an independent team that he initially formed back in 1939. Two years later, they joined the National Basketball League, and in 1949 Mr. Zollner provided the impetus for the merging of the NBL and the BAA to form the NBA. Plus, it was Mr. Z who gave me the chance to be a coach in the NBA.

So I was stunned and profoundly unhappy.

Mr. Zollner also told us that included in the deal with the new owner was the stipulation that I would be retained as coach and be signed to a new contract.

The new owner, Bill Davidson, had made his fortune heading a company that produced glass and fiberglass components for automobiles. In any event, after some bargaining and prompting from Mr. Coil, Mr. Davidson agreed to pay me a guaranteed, incentivized contract that could pay me $100,000 (worth $528,344 today) for each of the next three seasons.

From the start, I felt that Mr. Davidson and a minority owner, Oscar Feldman, were uncomfortable with me. For example, Mr. Davidson and I were in San Francisco for a preseason NBA meeting, and we were sitting at the same table in a nightclub. When the band started playing "Take the 'A' Train," I said, "That's a Duke Ellington tune."

Much to my surprise, Mr. Davidson responded vehemently. "No! No!" he shouted. "Ellington didn't write that song."

Even though I hadn't made that claim, Davidson continued attacking me like I was Attila the Hun. "No! No! It was Billy Strayhorn." Which was something that I already knew.

Then there was a press conference, the reason for which I don't remember. Feldman was there with his son. The local newspapers had greeted my hiring by saying I was "a smart guy" and other positives. When Feldman's son saw how politely the media questioned me at the conference, he said to his father, "Wow! He's got them mesmerized."

Feldman shrugged and said, "I have no idea why."

The message I continually got from those two owners was, "Why does this guy think he's so special?"

Which was something that I never felt.

Perhaps they felt they had been strong-armed into hiring me, and were antagonistic because I wasn't their hire. But maybe there was another, simpler, and more obvious reason. . . . Maybe they just weren't comfortable with a Black coach, and didn't mind letting me know it.

During the summer of 1974, Dave Bing, Don Adams, and Curtis Rowe all met with Mr. Davidson to have their existing contracts renegotiated. When Mr. Davidson turned them all down, Bing and Adams said they would hold out until their demands were met. Rowe eventually reported to training camp on time, but both Bing and Adams never showed up.

I believed that all three deserved raises, especially Adams. His effort and smarts on defense had been absolutely critical to our success. However, I felt that if Adams were granted a pay boost, Mr. Davidson would have to do the same for Bing and Rowe. I thought that this would never happen.

In any event, I thought it would be reasonable for me to assume that the momentum of the previous season would inspire everybody and that we had an excellent chance to at least be the Eastern Conference champions.

However, we had lost Stu Lantz in the latest expansion draft. Lantz wanted to be on the available list because he wanted to play with Pete Maravich in New Orleans. And Lantz got his wish.

I had no idea if Adams would ever play for the Pistons again, yet we were stacked at the forward positions with Bob Nash, Willie Norwood, Curtis Rowe, Trapp, and rookie Al Eberhard, our first-round pick (fifteenth overall) from Missouri. I also had the same doubt about Bing's future in Detroit, and with Lantz gone, I had to add two new guards to the team. One of these turned out to be 6′0″, 170-pound Eric Money, our second-round pick (thirty-third overall) from Arizona, who had the potential to become a dynamic scorer.

There were two candidates for the other guard spot: Billy Ligon, our tenth-round pick from Vanderbilt, who stayed on the roster until Bing eventually returned. And Mo Layton, who had bounced around the NBA with three teams in three seasons, plus one season in the ABA. Even though Layton was not a star player, I had tentatively penciled him onto the twelve-man roster that would open the season should Bing and Adams continue their holdouts. So when Bing and Adams began talking about returning, I cut Layton.

Layton was angry, but then I got upset when he called the league office and complained about being cut. That resulted in Simon Gourdine, the NBA's vice president (!) calling to have me explain why I had waived Layton.

Say what?

The call was amicable, but my anger was stoked even more.

I believed then, and still do, that the only reason for the call was that I was an African American coach. *Really!* One year later, John MacLeod (a white coach!) cut Layton before Phoenix began the season. And I can guarantee that nobody from the league office called MacLeod to find out why Layton had been cut.

So our 1974–75 season was buried before it began.

On the road, I often used the team's credit card to treat the players to dinner. My aim was to try and re-create a sense of togetherness. And this worked for a while.

Indeed, things looked promising when, despite the complaints about their respective financial situations, Bing and Rowe played hard and even stepped up their production. As a result, we were first in our division with a 30–20 record.

Still, there were some problems. Our defense continued operating at the same stifling level as the previous season. In fact, our points-against was the same 100.3. Our biggest letdown, however, was on offense—from averaging 104.4 to averaging 98.9 (which ranked us sixteenth in a seventeen-team league). Bing and Rowe were scoring more than they had in 1973–74, but Adams had a big drop-off.

In 1973–74, Adams's numbers were 10.3 points and 6.1 rebounds. Unlike Bing and Rowe, Adams never got over Mr. Davidson's refusal to increase his salary, and his continued grousing was a significant distraction. The decrease in his on-court energy resulted in his production shrinking to 6.1 points and 4.7 rebounds. Naturally, this led to a similar decrease in Adams's playing time.

I had to do something to try and save the season.

Mr. Coil and I discussed the possibilities, and a trade was proposed and accepted by New York. I hoped that sending a number-one draft pick to New York in exchange for Howard Porter would solve our offensive deficiencies.

In 1972, the 6'9", 220-pound Porter had been an All-American in his senior year at Villanova, and was immediately wooed by both the NBA and the ABA, with a resulting escalation in proffered contracts. Because NBA teams believed Porter would eventually sign with the ABA, the Bulls were reluctant to waste their first-round pick on him and eventually selected him in the second round as the thirty-second overall pick. Even so, they still had to outbid the ABA to get him to Chicago.

There was no question that although he was somewhat erratic, Porter was very talented. He could shoot, run, and sky, but was not an elite passer or defender. Perhaps that's why he had been dealt to New York, where he mostly gathered splinters on the bench. However, he had always brought his A-game whenever we had faced the Bulls.

Although Porter did take some games off, in forty-two games with us, he shot 50 percent, averaged 10.6 points, and was a big plus.

However, bringing in Porter turned the landslide into an avalanche and the avalanche into an earthquake. Because Bing, Rowe, and especially Adams now began to resent the big money Porter was getting. This discontent was contagious and was clearly reflected by the lack of on-court commitment evidenced by all the players. But when Adams so blatantly quit on me, I gave up waiting for him to come around, and the connection between the two of us was irrevocably broken.

Then Adams missed a team bus, and the conflict between us grew even hotter. So, with Mr. Coil's approval, I cut Adams in midseason, a move that his teammate and close friend Bing publicly criticized. For sure, Bing and I had our adversarial moments, but that often happens between coaches and players. Yet although I was hurt by Bing's public reaction, I took the hit and moved on.

From that point, there was no doubt in my mind that I had lost the team.

Things got worse as the season progressed. We finished the season going 10–22, and wound up at 40–42. We did manage to qualify for the playoffs, and faced off against a very good Seattle team that featured Donald "Slick" Watts, "Downtown" Freddie Brown, Archie "Shake and Bake" Clark, Spencer Haywood, and Tom Burleson. Nobody played well in our two losses in Seattle, but Dave Bing returned to form and was especially effective in Game 2 in Detroit, our only win in the series.

It should be noted, however, that years later Dave and I attended Earl Lloyd's wedding, where we had an honest man-to-man discussion and buried the hatchet—and not in each other! Subsequently we once again became close friends, and I campaigned for him during his successful run to become mayor of Detroit.

By the conclusion of that painful 1974–75 season, the foundation of our wonderful 52-win season was already cracked and crumbling.

Of course, I was (and still am) personally disturbed by the interference that the league office had subjected me to, but the one major factor that did us all in was . . . MONEY!

Even so, I had a blueprint, which I aimed to use to resurrect my team.

CHAPTER SIXTEEN

HOW BOB FERRY SHOWED ME THE WAY TO BUILD A CHAMPIONSHIP TEAM

Nowadays, teams can move instantly from the outhouse to the penthouse by the judicious signing of free agents. Back then, though, the climb took much longer and was much more complicated. As an example of how much the game has changed, here's how the Baltimore/Capital/Washington Bullets made their way from mediocrity to a championship.

Bob Ferry was the general manager and his first and most important move was consummated on June 23, 1972, when he traded Jack Marin along with "future considerations" (which meant that the Bullets would pay a major share of Marin's contract) to Houston in exchange for Elvin Hayes.

This deal ranks up there in league-changing importance with past trades involving Kareem's coming to the Lakers, Wilt's having the same new destination, and the Celtics getting Bill Russell.

Even so, I initially doubted that the trade would work out for the Bullets. My thought was that Hayes and Wes Unseld would get in each other's way. I was never more wrong.

Unseld would set screens, rebound, and occasionally hit an unopposed short jumper. Meanwhile, Hayes was a high-volume scorer in the low post, which forced the defense to pay close attention to him and subsequently resulted in open shots for the Bullets' trio of knock-down shooters—namely Archie Clark, Phil Chenier, and Mike Riordan.

But Ferry wasn't done.

The following season, the Bullets added Nick Weatherspoon, a high-jumping, high-scoring forward. Also Kevin Porter, a point guard who could fly into the lane at will and make accurate passes.

In 1974–75, their bench was fortified with the addition of Len "Truck" Robinson, Jimmy Jones, and Clem Haskins. A year later Dave Bing, and Kevin Grevey joined the team. The Bullets were on the verge of being a true championship contender in 1976–77 when Tom Henderson and Mitch Kupchak came on board.

Newcomers Charles Johnson and Larry Wright joined the fun in 1977–78, but the final piece to the championship puzzle was Bobby Dandridge. While the squad was loaded with veterans, Dandridge was the only player on the team who had a championship ring.

All of Ferry's long, patient maneuvers finally peaked when the Bullets beat Seattle to win the seventh game of the finals and the NBA championship on June 7, 1978. This was only sixteen days short of the sixth anniversary of the Marin-Hayes trade.

So I had a lot to do and, following Ferry's process, I looked to do in Detroit what he had done in Baltimore and I believed I had the time to do it all.

CHAPTER SEVENTEEN

THE BEGINNING OF THE END, AND THE BLOOD ON MY BACK

The calamitous 1975–76 season actually began in the locker room on April 12, 1975, right after the Sonics beat us in the deciding third game of that series. That's when Mr. Davidson approached me and said that Dave Bing had to be traded. It seems that in addition to Bing's sub-par play, his agent was still involved in disagreements with Mr. Davidson about contractual renegotiations. Mr. Davidson was simply fed up with Bing.

I reluctantly agreed to trade Bing, my only request being that I seek out and make the final decision on whichever player we might get in exchange. Mr. Davidson had no problem with this. Nor did Oscar Feldman, who was a co-owner of the team and had also replaced Mr. Coil as general manager.

My ambition was to rebuild the team around Bob Lanier. My model was what Bob Ferry had done with the Bullets after obtaining Elvin Hayes and making him the centerpiece of the team's future.

So I called several general managers to see who might be available. I had originally set my sights on Chicago's Norm Van Lier, but Dick Motta wouldn't part with him.

After much investigation, I settled on Kevin Porter, a super-quick, pass-first point guard with the Bullets. Porter wanted out of Washington because the Bullets wouldn't pay him what he deserved.

And he deserved plenty.

Many players are fast while running without the ball, but Porter was faster with the ball than anybody I'd ever seen since Randy Smith, Nate "Tiny" Archibald, and maybe Guy Rodgers, plus, like them, KP could finish in a crowd. Porter's sleight-of-hand with the ball while at full speed was simply amazing. But he could also score when he had to, as evidenced by his performance in the conference finals against the Celtics the previous season. Porter was a key element in Washington's winning as a result of his averaging 25 points throughout the six games. And the topper for me was that he made all of his teammates better.

So the trade was made, and I looked forward to having us playing at the speedball pace that Porter set.

Ah, what might have been. . . .

During the off-season I also decided that I needed an experienced assistant coach. My first choice was Rod Thorn, who was currently an assistant to Kevin Loughery with the Nets. Rod flew to Detroit, we had a terrific interview, and he said, "Let me get back to you." But he was then offered and accepted the head coaching position with the ABA's St. Louis Spirits, a loaded team that was good enough to have been a force in the NBA.

My next choice was Gene "Bumper" Tormohlen, who was assisting Cotton Fitzsimmons in Atlanta. Gene turned me down, saying he was committed to the Hawks.

Through the years, I had maintained my connection with Haskell Cohen. Even so, I was surprised when he called me.

I was even more surprised when he said that he'd heard I was looking for an assistant coach. "There's Herb Brown, Larry's brother, who's available. He's been coaching and winning championships in Israel and he knows the pro game. You'd be doing me a great favor if you hired Herb, because I owe him some money."

"Okay. I'll get him to Detroit, interview him. Then let you know."

Herb was very "charming," and I was impressed when I saw he understood how I wanted to utilize Kevin Porter to speed up the offense. So I hired him.

Herb had not been on my list and I didn't know him from Adam's cat. I should have called Larry, who, even though we didn't have a real close connection, had been my teammate in Virginia. However, I doubt that Larry would have dissuaded me from hiring his brother.

Who I really should have contacted was Doug Moe, another Squires' teammate, a close friend of Larry's, and someone who could have given me the straight skinny on Herb.

But doing a solid for Haskell seemed sufficient.

Yet I was very uncomfortable when, after our interview, Herb conferred with Oscar Feldman in his office. Something was wrong about this. I had been hired by Mr. Zollner, and Herb was the new owners' first coaching hire, and was apparently selling himself as Feldman's guy.

In any event, Herb was really good during training camp. He was teaching proper ball placement, the Celtics' fastbreak where the wings crossed at the endline, KP stopping at either foul line extended to give an easily identifiable lane for the trailers to use, and generally refining how/where/why everybody else should skedaddle when Porter was triggering the break.

I was initially encouraged because Herb seemed to be a good fit. The only problem was that he always seemed to be whispering in somebody's ear. I was uneasy with this, but I overlooked it.

Much more disturbing was something that happened during a preseason game against the Lakers in Ohio: Herb began standing up to yell out plays and correct the players' movements. *What the hell was that?*

Later I figured out that he was putting on a show for the owners, showing that he was really the brains of the operation and that he was responsible for any success the team had.

I should have told him to sit his ass down. If I needed him, I'd summon him. But I said nothing, yet I never felt he had my back. In fact, I later discovered that he occasionally had brunch at Feldman's house.

In any case, later that same night I got a call from Jerry Green, a sportswriter for one of the Detroit newspapers. "Ray, who's coaching the team?"

"I'll deal with it."

But I didn't. Mainly because we were winning.

A big reason for our success was that KP always studied our opponents. How did they tend to react on defense against fastbreaks? Did they stay with their man? Run to the basket? Pick up the first players who crossed the timeline? So he knew which-and-where teammates would be open. As a result our running game was devastating.

And if KP was the motor, Lanier was the anchor because he could post up and also shoot from anywhere up to twenty feet. Out there, Bob could make some kind of *boomp boomp* move, then pull and shoot, which meant that guys like Kareem and

Thurmond had a difficult time guarding him so far from the basket.

Curtis Rowe could run with the guards, and do so with the elegance of a gazelle. John "Crash" Mengelt filled a wing whenever we ran and filled the basket when he shot his jumper. Al Eberhard was an amazing spot shooter who could play a whole game, never dribble, and still average double figures.

We were 14–10, in first place in the division, and involved in a tough game at Golden State when suddenly, late in the first quarter, Kevin Porter went down. Nobody touched him, his feet weren't tangled, so it seemed to be some irregularity in the floor that got him. He was curled up and in extreme pain.

I was in shock. Worried first and foremost about KP, and then about the team.

I was still stunned when, a few minutes later, John Mengelt also collapsed.

WHAT? THIS WAS UNBELIEVABLE!

Turned out that both had suffered knee injuries. Mengelt returned to the team after I was history, but KP needed surgery. The rest of the season was a nightmare.

My starting backcourt became Chris Ford, who was not a runner, and Eric Money, a terrific player but more of a scorer than a passer. There were no adequate backups, so sometimes I had to play these guys more than 45 minutes every game.

Of course we started losing, and it was clear to me that I was in an extremely shaky position.

Our record was now 17–25, and we had just lost a tough home game against the Knicks on a Saturday night. Afterward, I was standing outside the locker room, as I usually did, to make sure that all the players had gone inside before I entered to give my postgame talk. While I was out there, Feldman walked right past me and into the room without saying a word. I followed him and said that I'd welcome him in here but only after I spoke to the team.

Feldman's response was, "No, wait outside." So I went back out into the hall.

A few minutes later, Feldman came out and said, "Herb explained to me why I shouldn't be in there until you were finished." Then he left.

And I knew that I was done.

I went inside, thanked the players for their effort, packed up my stuff, and left.

The next morning, I got a call from a TV newsman. "Ray, these guys are getting ready to fire you." Which was certainly not news to me.

I hadn't yet heard anything from management, so I showed up at 7:00 on Monday night for a scheduled practice session. While the players were warming up, Mr. Davidson, Feldman, and Herb Tyner, the three principal owners, came into the gym.

Now, I may have been born at night, but not last night.

We all went into the locker room where Mr. Davidson said the words that were always said when the pink slip was being handed over: "We're going to make a change."

But the "chauffeur" spoke up. "Why are you firing me?"

"Because of a lack of communication," Mr. Davidson said.

"Lack of communication with who?"

"The players, the front office, and three of us owners."

"Don't bullshine me," I said. "Here's your whistle." Which I tossed on a table.

Then I went upstairs and told the players, "I'm out." I thanked them again for their efforts, and we shook hands.

The opera had played out to its not-so-grand finale, and the Fat Lady was singing.

Two days later, Herb called me to ask if I had any trades in the works. "No," I said, then quickly hung up.

Once he took over, Herb cut Lindsay Hairston, a forward I thought had the potential to be outstanding, and Earl Williams, a backup center. And he brought in Henry Dickerson and Roger Brown, two guys who had played for him in Israel.

With Herb in charge and everybody healthy, the team went 19–21. For sure, they did somewhat better, but there was no whoop-dee-do improvement. They did make the playoffs, however, and faced Milwaukee in the first round. By this time, Kareem and Oscar were gone, so while the Bucks were still a good squad—led by Bobby Dandridge, Elmore Smith, and Brian Winters—they weren't the elite team they once were. Still, it was a mild surprise when the Pistons beat Milwaukee in three games. They then lost to Golden State in six games.

As for me, I stayed home in Detroit and quickly got two calls: The first was to coach for the summer in Puerto Rico, which several NBA coaches had already done—but I turned the offer down.

I did accept the second job offer, however—to coach at Eastern Michigan University.

PART FOUR

CHAPTER EIGHTEEN

ABRACADABRA, AND THE NBA FLIES HIGH

When Earvin "Magic" Johnson and Larry Bird both made their NBA debuts at the beginning of the 1979–80 season, the most-watched televised sports in America were (in order of popularity):

Major League baseball

Professional football

Hockey (fourteen of the seventeen teams were situated in the States)

College basketball

College football

Indeed, whenever the media covered basketball, the NBA was rarely in the discussions. The reputations of players were mostly made in NCAA competition, especially in the nationally televised season-ending championship tournaments. The NBA was sometimes followed by college fans to discover the professional fate of such Final Four MVPs as Paul Hogue (Cincinnati, 1962), Art Heyman (Duke, 1963), Hal Lear (Temple, 1956), B. H. Born (Kansas, 1953), plus Jerry Lucas, Jerry West, Wilt, and Russ. Some of these guys turned out to be busts, while others became Hall-of-Famers. But the emergence of

Johnson and Bird in "The Dance" made this a must-see event for even casual basketball fans.

In fact, for a variety of other reasons, Magic and Bird turbo-charged the appeal, and profitability, of virtually every aspect of the NBA. These days, the nationwide popularity of the NBA has surpassed hockey as well as both collegiate sports. NBA franchises are now worth mega-millions, the league made nearly $1.5B in sponsorship revenues during the 2020–21 season, and virtually every star player is paid upward of $20M.

One reason why Magic and Bird were such celebrities was that they both had especially endearing qualities, even though very different from each other.

Johnson was born in Lansing, Michigan, which was largely farm country, and had been drafted from Michigan State in East Lansing. Yet when he became a Laker, he quickly transformed himself into a city-wise denizen of the Magic City. It should be noted that the first hoop-time "Magic" was Earl Monroe, who was also known as "Black Magic."

Bird, on the other hand, was born and raised in French Lick, Indiana, and was regularly called "The Hick from French Lick." It took Bird many years to become a willing and even semi-eloquent public interview.

Bird and Johnson disliked each other at first. Why wouldn't they, when the media was continually asking, "Who's better?"

Though they rarely if ever guarded each other, Magic's Lakers and Bird's Celtics faced off eighteen times in regular-season play as well as nineteen times in playoffs. If the results seem lopsided, keep in mind that while Boston's front line of Bird, McHale, and Parish was one of the best ever, the Lakers could counter with James "Big Game James" Worthy, Jamaal Wilkes, plus Kareem and his unstoppable Sky Hook.

So, Magic's per-game numbers in LA's eleven regular-season wins over Boston included 19.4 points, 6.8 rebounds, and 11.5 assists.

For Bird in Boston's 7 wins: 21.7 points, 10.9 rebounds, and 6.2 assists per game.

Magic's Lakers won two championships in direct competition with Bird's Celtics (1985 and 1987), and they, in turn, beat LA in the Finals only once (1984).

In the Lakers-Celtics playoff games, Magic and Company won 11 times, with Johnson averaging 20.7 points, 7.3 rebounds, and 13.5 assists.

Compare that with Bird in Boston's eight victories, 25.3 points, 11.1 rebounds, and 4.6 assists.

Of course, no one player can single-handedly defeat another team. Yet it's obvious that both Magic and Bird were at their best when their teams met.

Their games were also different:

Both stood 6′9″, and were two-time college All-Americans, but where Magic was a forward-sized point guard, Bird was a slightly oversized small forward.

Magic could totally control the ball while running at full speed (and was faster than Bird). His unusual size enabled him to see over his defenders and to scan all the action in front of him, which was one reason why his passwork was so incredible. Equally incredible was his ability to finish on the run in heavy traffic with hooks, flips, dunks, and shots that can't be categorized. Magic's decision-making was also fantastic and, like an overgrown Kevin Porter, he made better players of all his teammates

If Magic wasn't a naturally gifted defender, he compensated by using his intelligence to study his opponents, and by playing the passing and cutting angles. Rather than having to defend the smaller, quicker point guards, Magic usually took on the opponent's shooting guard while Byron Scott or Michael Cooper defended the points. Magic's go-to outside shot was the stab, and was good enough to keep defenses honest.

However, Magic needed the right coach to maximize his special talents. At the start of his rookie season (1979–80), the Lakers were coached by Jack McKinney, who suffered a severe bicycle accident early in the season and was succeeded by Paul Westhead. In one of the most memorable games in NBA history, the twenty-year-old Magic replaced the injured Kareem Abdul-Jabbar in the sixth and last game of the Finals. He recorded 42 points, 15 rebounds, and 7 assists in leading Los Angeles to the championship.

Yet the following season under Westhead proved to be a profound disappointment. After finishing with a record of 54–28, the Lakers unexpectedly lost an opening best-of-three-games playoff series to the Houston Rockets. I don't know all the specifics, but I do know that's when the players turned against Westhead. So, after commencing the 1981–82 season at 7–4, Westhead was fired and the Lakers' new leader was Pat Riley.

Riley was a veteran of nine NBA seasons (1967–76)—two with San Diego, seven-plus with the Lakers, and a partial season with Phoenix. He'd been a hard-nosed bench player in 1972 when the Lakers were NBA champs. But when he took over as the team's coach, he was slicker than thou. With his Armani suits, his glowing tan, his resemblance to Kirk Douglas and unrelenting glamour, Riley was the epitome of a Hollywood superstar. And he was a really good coach. He traded Norm Nixon, Magic's only rival for dominant ball time, for Byron Scott (who was mostly a catch-and-shoot guy). That gave

Magic free rein to up the tempo to warp speed, and thereby engineered what became known as "Showtime" in LA.

Bird was a small forward who could play power forward against some opponents. He could score in multiple ways: in the low post, facing-up an opponent, finding layups in heavy traffic, or bagging 3-pointers. Like Magic, Bird was an exceptional passer, plus he could run with the guards and rebound with the bigs. If Bird wasn't a defensive stopper, he did play effective team defense. Just as crucial, Bird didn't buy into the predominant racial bias in Boston.

Geography was another factor.

The special boost that Magic and Bird gave to the NBA was rooted in the rivalry between Boston on the East Coast and Los Angeles on the West Coast. This type of intense coast-to-coast rivalry between two teams and two transcendent players had not been seen previously in the NBA.

Wilt-versus-Russ was mostly confined to the Northeast—Philly and Boston—and there were no formidable rivalries in the West. An older Wilt did have several confrontations (from 1969 to 1973) when the young Abdul-Jabbar was with the Milwaukee Bucks. Yet the Bucks played in flyover territory, in a city that was definitely not a major metropolis. That's why this was never a commercially popular rivalry, and didn't last very long either.

Also, once Wilt retired in 1973, the 7′2″ Kareem was unquestionably the most gifted center in the league. Yet he faced talented rival big men like Willis Reed (6′10″) and Bob Lanier (6′11″), who were all too small to effectively limit Kareem's dominance.

Dave Cowens was "only" 6′9″, yet in 1974 he was a major factor in the Celtics beating Kareem's Milwaukee Bucks for the NBA championship. Boston was a sprint team that featured speedsters like John Havlicek, Paul Westphal, Jo Jo White, and Art Williams. And Cowens could not only out-quick Kareem, but he didn't stop running until he got back to the hotel.

Another aspect of the Magic-Bird rivalry in the NBA was the fact that they had previously been rivals in college.

Wilt and Russell, on the other hand, had no significant rivals in college: When Wilt was at Kansas, his most celebrated oppo-nent was Lennie Rosenbluth from North Carolina, who later played only sparingly in the NBA, averaging a mere 4.2 points per game during his two seasons with Philadelphia (1957–59). Similarly, when Russ was at the University of San Francisco (USF), his primary rivals were largely unknown because USF's home games were never televised live in the East, where the media was centered. Furthermore, back then the NCAA Final Four contests were only televised on delayed tape.

It's well known that Boston was a haven for white players and a historical nightmare for Black players, while Los Angeles was a multicultural city. But the racial aspect of the Celtic-Lakers competition did not a factor into the public's fascination with their rivalry.

There's no doubt that Bird versus Magic and Boston versus Los Angeles revived the NBA. Game attendance as well as TV ratings sky-rocketed. Even the most casual Kansas City Kings' fans wanted to see Bird and Magic compete. Previously, the NBA's game results and doings had mostly been available only in local newspapers. But now the Lakers' home games against Boston were shown live, which even attracted a con-siderable number of viewers when telecast at 10:30 p.m. in the East. Plus, when the Celtics hosted the Lakers, many of those games were broadcast on ABC-TV on primetime weekend afternoons.

Think of the competitions between the New York Yankees and the Boston Red Sox. Or the Brooklyn/LA Dodgers and the New York/San Francisco Giants. Magic vs. Bird was a financial, cultural, race-obscuring bonanza.

Of course, the NBA's publicity machine worked overtime to highlight and cash in on basketball's version of the New Deal. So did Converse, which shot sneaker commercials with both Magic and Bird and issued special-edition Converse Weapons featuring their autographs.

Bird and Magic may not ever have been super popular with their teammates, but they were always highly respected.

There was still another important difference in the early NBA careers of Magic and Bird:

The Black player's initial NBA contract paid him $460,000 for each of five years.

The white player's initial NBA contract paid him $650,000 for each of five years.

It should be noted that, for the 1978–79 season, while playing for Philadelphia, Moses Malone had received the first million dollar deal. The second-highest player behind Malone was Kareem, with $825,000.

Then, for the 1984–85 season, Magic's and Bird's contracts both exploded. Bird's new deal was worth $1.8M, and increased in significant amounts thereafter. At the same time, Magic signed a deal that would pay him a million dollars for each of the next twenty-five years. Whatever the initial discrepancy between the earnings of the two players, it was eventually rectified. Because Magic's twenty-five-year contract was boosted seven times over the course of his thirteen active seasons, his average season's salary came to $2.8M and considerable change. Over his twelve active seasons, Bird averaged $1.85M.

In any event, the respect paid to Bird and Magic financially, together with the emergence of the players' union, was instrumental in the multi-million dollar player contracts that soon became routine.

To this day, Magic and Bird are still irrevocably linked together, and the crucial role they jointly played in boosting the appeal of the NBA should never be forgotten.

Charles Barkley agrees: "Magic Johnson and Larry Bird are the two most important people in NBA history. If it weren't for these guys, the NBA wouldn't be what it is today."

Unfortunately, when Bird (1992) and Magic (1996) hung up their sneakers, the allure of their rivalry could not be equaled. Not even Julius in Philly versus Bill Walton in Portland ever quite aroused the same interest.

What eventually renewed the NBA's popularity wasn't a rivalry this time but the NBA's focus on the fantastic individual talent of His Airness, which brought Bulls games to prime time. Michael Jordan was given the stage, and the Nike commercials that he appeared in with Spike Lee made MJ even more of cultural icon. The NBA's newfound focus on superstars led to the celebration of guys like Charles Barkley, Patrick Ewing, David Robinson, Hakeem Olajuwon, Dominique Wilkins, Karl Malone, and Clyde Drexler. Nowadays, the league's TV megastar is LeBron, closely trailed by Stephen Curry.

The most publicized team/city rivalry that temporarily equaled the days of Magic-Bird were the over-the-top brutal confrontations between MJ's Bulls and the Pistons' Bad Boys.

Some of the Bad Boys (most notably Rick Mahorn, Bill Laimbeer, and Dennis Rodman) prided themselves on being tough guys. While Detroit is, and always has been, primarily a baseball/football/hockey town, the Pistons drew SRO crowds for their two championship seasons. Even though the Palace at Auburn was a cross-highway arena that was situated in a wealthy neighborhood about an hour's drive from Detroit, it was one of the finest arenas in the NBA.

However, as the Pistons faded into mediocrity, the Palace was torn down. In 2014 in partnership with the Detroit Red Wings, ground was broken in Center City to construct not only Little Caesars Arena (LCA) but an entire neighborhood of bars, nightclubs, and restaurants. When the LCA opened in 2017, Detroiters were enabled to have easy access to both teams' home games.

Since I was deeply involved with pro basketball for fifteen years—nine as an NBA player, two playing in the ABA, and coaching the Pistons for four years—I would be remiss if I failed to mention some of the players who were among the greatest people I've ever had the pleasure and honor to befriend and admire.

There's Julius, an erudite individual who was iconic off the court as well as on the court. For example, after losses or games when he hadn't played up to his standards, Julius never hid in the trainers' room. Instead, he sat at his locker and spoke to every single media person who approached him. Which was why Julius was usually the last player out of the locker room.

Walt Bellamy was a good friend through the years. There's been a tendency to downgrade his accomplishments, even though he averaged nearly 30 points and 20 rebounds going against Wilt and Russ.

Speaking of Russ, in private he's an incredibly intelligent and compassionate person.

John "Rabbit" Barnhill was my roomie in Baltimore. He had learned the intricacies of the game at Tennessee A&I under the great John McLendon, who was one of the early great Black coaches. No wonder Barnhill had such a vast knowledge of the game. In addition, he was a great guy and a close buddy through the years.

I always loved playing against Rudy "Deuce" LaRusso. He was up there with Gus Johnson, Dave DeBusschere, and Tom Meschery as being great players at both ends of the court. All of these guys were highly competitive without being dirty. Thus, I had a special on-court relationship with Rudy that always brought out the best in me.

Then there was Dick "Skull" Barnett, an extremely intelligent guy whose top-notch defense was usually overlooked.

I've already expressed my appreciation of Earl Lloyd and Dave Bing.

Also among the best people I've ever met are John Havlicek and Willis Reed.

There are so many others, but to name them all would take up a long, separate chapter.

In March 1980, however, my attention was diverted from the NBA to my new career—coaching collegiate basketball.

CHAPTER NINETEEN

SAME GAME, NEW RULES

Eastern Michigan University (EMU) is situated on 460 acres in Ypsilanti and, at the time I was there, had an overall student population of about twenty thousand. The basketball coach had been Al Freund, a really nice man who hadn't come close to a winning season. Over his five-year tenure, the team was 36–69. Al faced one major problem that prevented any chance of success: EMU moved from Division 2 to Division 1 in his last season. That meant that his 1975–76 schedule included several powerhouse opponents. When he was fired at the end of that season, the job was open.

Dr. Bob Sims was an influential alumnus of EMU, who was in the school's Hall of Fame for his accomplishments starring in both basketball and track. Because we were good friends, Bob told the president that he could probably convince me to be their next coach. His suggestion was met with enthusiasm. As a result, I soon met with James Brickley, EMU's president, and Dr. Eugene Smith, who was the first African American athletic director in Division 1 history. We all quickly agreed that I was right for the job.

I'd never had an agent as either a professional player or a coach, so I had no idea how to negotiate a contract. Nor did I know what the other coaches at EMU were paid. I only knew that I was the sole Black coach in the athletic department and that the budget for the basketball coach ranged from $21,000 to $24,000. Although I did receive the max (worth $76,188 today), I knew I was being underpaid, but I didn't have any other options that would keep me in basketball.

I'd heard that too many colleges were reluctant to pay African American coaches what they were worth. In retrospect, I think I've figured out why. It's because white executives believed that white employees require a higher standard of living than Black employees. Unfortunately, this distorted and racially prejudiced practice remains in effect in too many work situations even today.

In any event, the EMU deal included four guaranteed years with something like a 75 percent cost-of-living increase added every year. Since I also had what the Pistons paid me for the remaining year of my contract with them, I had a big enough stash.

I was a thirty-six-year-old "fish out of water," so I didn't realize that I could have asked the school to also provide living quarters. I made no demands, so all I was given was a car. I already had a Cadillac Seville for my own personal use, so I chose a Chevy van because I knew I'd need it to transport my players.

Before I got the job, I was paying $800 a month to rent a nice-enough two-bedroom apartment in a lakeside development, where the view was the main attraction. Another plus was that it was only a 15-minute drive from the campus. Then, once I'd completed my first season at EMU and believed I'd be there for the long term, I bought a condo.

Before I even began the job, when I first arrived and my hiring and salary were posted in the local media, the football coach suddenly resigned. We had a brief conversation before he left in which he said, "It's not your fault that I resigned. I did it because of how the university views me and my program." I had just gotten there, so, not even close to being an insider yet, I knew nothing about his program and understood the gist of his complaint but none of the specifics. It was a vague hint of things to come.

Bob Fenton was a Detroit-based sports attorney who represented big-time athletes like Mickey Lolich and Al Kaline. Bob was also well connected with local and state political leaders and happened to be a good friend of mine. During my first year at EMU, Bob arranged for me to write a weekly column for *The Detroit News*. I wrote almost exclusively about sports, both local and national, and at my own expense I traveled to New York City to witness the third Ali-Norton fight. Perhaps the most important column I wrote, however, was to sympathize with a teachers' strike in Detroit.

I also did a weekly 15-minute prime-time radio show on WJR where, as a onetime Pistons' player and coach, I only discussed basketball. Again, as something of a local celebrity, I made the rounds of the rubber-chicken circuit. My itinerary was to look at the chicken, make my speech, then go to a restaurant for dinner.

The EMU season was over when I signed on in March, but the high school state championship tournament was under way. So my initial job as coach was to scout high school kids who were playing in the tournament and also in summer leagues. I enjoyed just watching them play, yet I had to study the relevant NCAA rules and learn them in a hurry. When could I talk to the kids? What could I say to them? When could I visit them at their homes?

It turned out that recruiting was a brutal process.

The EMU team had graduated three players, so I had three scholarships to offer. David "Smokey" Gaines was the assistant basketball coach at the University of Detroit and he told me that a lot of kids I'd try to recruit would be using me as a fallback in case they couldn't get the offer they wanted from the school they really wanted to go to. However, under no circumstances should I ever lie to them.

And Smokey was right on. Many of the kids bullshined me six ways from Sunday, saying how much they liked the prospect of going to EMU. As Smokey said, they were just hedging their bets. I learned that the best way to get to the truth was to speak to the kids with their parent on hand. "Oh, no, Johnny. You said that you really want to go to. . . ." There were many times when the truth broke my heart.

There was one 6'11" kid I was trying to sign who was All-State. Dr. Sims and I were in his living room and were practically kissing his butt. "If you come to EMU," I said, "we can build a team around you." The kid and his parents were nodding with enthusiasm, when suddenly his bother came home from work and said, "He only wants to play in warm weather." I don't remember exactly where he wound up, but he never made much of an impact, wherever it was.

Yet most kids were totally honest.

Despite having to compete with Michigan and Michigan State, I sought to recruit the most elite high school players in the area. They included Magic Johnson, who quickly informed me that he was going to Michigan State. Also two more future NBA players—Walker D. Russell and Bob Elliott—who likewise put me straight right away as to what college they had already decided to attend.

So while I could usually rely on a kid's telling the truth in front of his parents, the parents themselves quite often presented a different problem. There I'd be, sitting in their living room, and they'd swear that their kid was the next Bob Lanier or the next Dave Bing. Really! I was thinking about how I could make their kid a better player, while they were already thinking about the NBA. I knew that these folks loved and were proud of their kids, but none of them had any idea of how truly great even the worst NBA players are. I was bemused but kept my mouth shut.

I did take a look at three players from the same high school— Eric Money, Robert "Bubbles" Hawkins, and Coniel "Popcorn" Norman. However, it was immediately apparent that their quickness, elevation, and sheer talent destined them to play for some major college and then in the NBA. Which they all did.

I should have recruited second-line kids whose game I could develop over four years. But, coming from the pros, I was attracted to top-notch talent.

Also, although I knew that there were other schools making their recruiting pitches, I had no idea what those pitches were. Instead of my opponent being right in front of me, I was competing against shadows and whispers in the wind.

Everything considered, having to recruit high school kids, although necessary, was a horrible way to have to begin my new career. I couldn't wait to get into the gym and actually start coaching. Until then, what could my recruiting pitch be?

Dr. Eugene Smith was my mentor and guided me through the tangle of NCAA rules; he even accompanied me on most of my recruiting efforts. Early on, we had a sit-down to discuss what we could legally offer potential recruits. Free room and board. Free tuition. The team's scheduled road trip to Las Vegas this season, then New Orleans the following year. Maybe some part-time on-campus job cutting the grass on the baseball field, or drawing the lines on the football field. The kid would get a fair chance to earn his playing time. Dr. Smith was a great guy who always kept his promises to me, and we had a terrific relationship.

But ... he hired me in March, then was gone in June. Although he had cut the athletic department's budget to the bone, he was given an ultimatum by the administration: Cut it some more, or resign. Unfortunately, he chose the latter option. His departure left me with nobody to provide support or advice about how to navigate the NCAA rule book, or how to properly and effectively do my new job. I was totally on my own. (Nowadays, newly hired coaches in most colleges hire an assistant who's an expert in the relevant rules.)

An interim athletic director (AD) had the job for a short time, but then it was given to Alex Agase. An NFL veteran and onetime football coach, Agase had had great success at Northwestern University. Unfortunately, we never got along.

I had been recruiting a really good player from Kentucky and Dr. Smith made a promise that we would *try* to schedule a game at Kentucky Wesleyan so his parents could see him play. Before this could happen, the kid came to EMU anyway, so Agase put the whole idea on the back burner.

Okay. I accepted that.

But I did have a conflict with Agase over a more serious scheduling problem that really aggravated me. His predecessor, Dr. Smith, had contractually arranged a home-and-home series with Michigan State. We played at Michigan State the season I was hired, and lost on a last-second shot that I believed was made after the horn sounded.

"Okay," I said to myself as I walked to the locker room, "we'll get them next year when they come to us."

A contract had been signed, and the scheduled date for this game was November 15. By then Magic would be an entering freshman and playing for the Spartans, so the game would be a surefire sellout at our home court in the Bowen Field House.

When I was going over our schedule for that following season, I called Jud Heathcote, Michigan State's coach. He said, "A game at your place? I don't know anything about that. Anyway, we're definitely not going down there."

I guessed that, with the expectation that Magic would be a huge draw, they had replaced us with a home game against a more glamorous opponent. I asked Agase about the situation and he said he had never seen the contract. I did a deep dive and eventually found the paperwork, but unfortunately it was too late by then. Nonetheless, there was the proof: We had been rudely disrespected by Michigan State.

When I told Agase that I'd found the contract, he asked to see it, so I handed it over to him. I watched as he took it and put it into a desk drawer. The outcome was that we never did host Michigan State and, since I hadn't made a copy, I never saw the contract again.

I wasn't Agase's hire, so maybe that's why he was constantly busting my chops about not following the NCAA recruiting rules diligently enough. Even more annoying was the dismissive attitude he showed toward me.

I'd often see Bob Fenton around and about. "How's it going?" he'd usually ask.

At some point, I complained to Bob about how much (and how, I thought, unfairly) the new AD was on my case about the rules. I thought this was a confidential conversation, but

Bob and President Brickley were old friends, so Bob shared my complaint with him.

I was then summoned to have lunch with Bob and President Brickley, where I was asked to repeat my concern about Agase. I couldn't really refuse, so I went through the whole deal again.

Okay. I thought that it was a minor matter and would soon be forgotten, so I went along my merry way. However, several months later I learned that President Brickley had passed along my comments to Agase.

Agase had been a football coach, right? Those guys are usually devoted to a chain of command with a militaristic passion. Since I had gone over his head, Agase now had a solid reason to treat me like crap.

Looking back, I came to understand that Agase was right and I was wrong in this case. If I'd had a beef, I should have gone straight to my immediate boss, which was Agase.

From then on, in some subtle and some more direct ways, Agase's treatment of me got worse. For example, we'd be at some social gathering, involved in a group conversation. I'd relate what I thought was an interesting incident, to which Agase would abruptly interject, "No. That's not what happened. Let me tell you what really happened." Then he'd repeat the story exactly as I'd told it.

Not only that but, on at least one occasion, Agase held a meeting with one of my assistants without inviting me. I had no idea what the motive of either of these two guys was.

With one thing after another, I began to seriously understand that I really didn't belong at EMU.

President Brickley had believed that since I had been the NBA Coach of the Year, hiring me would give a significant boost to the prestige of the basketball program. So at least he was in my corner. However, he left EMU after my second season because he was summoned to resume his old job as lieutenant governor of Michigan. That left me with no allies. Just me and Agase, with our mutual dislike.

Things weren't much better on the court. Even with the recruits who did sign up, my first season at EMU was not very enjoyable. We finished at 9–18, and I was amazed at how biased the referees were when we were on the road.

The worst jobbing I can remember was when we played the University of Nevada at Las Vegas (UNLV) in the opening game of a weekend tournament there. In virtually all road games, the refs were local guys, and getting jobbed was to be expected. So there was Jerry Tarkanian's squad with four All-Americans on the floor, and kicking our butts every which way.

Okay. No surprise.

There I was, sitting on the bench quietly dealing with getting blown out, when right in front of me, the ball bounced off one of the home team's player's legs and went out of bounds. There was no doubt about what had happened. The 100 percent call should have been our ball. But even though the nearest ref was out of position, he gave the possession to UNLV.

So I stood up and yelled at Tarkanian. "Hey, it's not enough that you're killing us, your refs have to make crazy calls like that?" Instead of responding, he took another bite at his towel.

What was just as frustrating was our getting jobbed at home games. Most refs instinctively favor the better of the two teams. Plus, we didn't have the talent to overcome bad calls. Only one of my players, Bob Riddle, was ever drafted by an NBA team. He was the last cut of the Cavs, then quit basketball and entered what's called "civilian life."

This unfair treatment by the whistle-tooters continued throughout my time at EMU.

Another factor in our poor record was that we played the likes of Michigan, Michigan State, UNLV, DePaul, Arizona, and New Orleans on the road. These Top Twenty schools wanted to play us in order to boost their records and straighten out their player rotations before their conference games began. And why did we want to get our butts mercilessly kicked? For the ample guaranteed money we'd get.

Then, in my third season, I made what was perceived by Agase (but not by me) as an egregious mistake. This is what eventually got me fired.

When I played at the University of Portland, the school had paid for me to fly home to Philly during the Christmas break. This was totally against NCAA rules, but I was nineteen years old and knew nothing about any of the organization's restrictions. All I knew was that I was given a wonderful opportunity to spend the holiday with my family.

During the spring and summer of 1977, prior to my third season at EMU, I was recruiting a young man whose mother lived in Baltimore. During our discussion, he asked if it would be possible for the school to pay for him to fly to Baltimore during the Christmas break. I said that I'd look into it.

There was a senior from Brooklyn on my team who came to me before that same season to say that he hadn't seen his mom in three years and to ask if he, too, could get home over the Christmas break on EMU's dime. I told him, as well, that I'd look into the possibility.

By now I knew the rules, of course, but I decided to go ahead and arrange for both of them to spend part of the holiday back home. I took the money for the tickets from the basketball team's Holiday Fund, which is something I shouldn't have done. But for us, the Christmas break was only about six days, during which the campus would be almost completely shut down. The dorms would be open, but the cafeteria would be closed. The players from Detroit had an easy time getting home, but the others would be stuck on campus. All the players, according to their needs, were supposed to be given money from this fund to pay for transportation, but only to Detroit and other local destinations. So I was planning to return the money to the fund ASAP, and to do so from my own pocket, but practice and then games restarted before I had the chance to do so. What I should have done was to put the tickets on my personal credit card. Or else I should have gone to Agase beforehand to alert him to my plan.

In any case, in my own naivete, I didn't think that what I'd done was such a big deal. No harm, no foul. Plus, I would never want to fail to provide any of my players with extracurricular assistance if I had the chance. Never. So I had no regrets about the situation. Back then, and to this day, I never feel bad about trying to help somebody. Anybody.

But when the news got to Agase, he called me on the carpet. I found out later that one of my assistants and one of the school's regents had leaked the whole thing to him.

"We need to address this situation," Agase said, "because the other kids got short-changed on their Holiday Fund payments."

"Yes, You're right. I'll write a check to replace that money. For what? Four-fifty? No problem."

Which I did, and the kids who were shorted soon got their payments squared away.

I had one more thing to say to Agase: "I just wanted to help those two kids. I didn't want them to fall."

Agase's response was, "Let them fall."

So I apologized to Agase and to each of the kids. Okay, I thought. That was the end of that, and whatever would happen would happen.

Agase didn't fire me (yet!) and I went about living my life and preparing for the following season. The only difference being that was I tired of dealing with all the nonsense, I couldn't hide my frustration, and my sense of being the wrong person in the wrong place at the wrong time increased.

Routine institutional racism plagued our culture. And though I had certainly made mistakes in how I had handled helping out my players, I couldn't avoid asking myself if Agase would have been more agreeable if I were a white coach.

I later discovered that he started approaching other coaches after that Christmas episode. Then, late in my third and last season at EMU, I got the message loud and clear.

Smokey Gaines was the first to tell me that Agase was looking to get rid of me. Then I got a visit from Mick McCabe, an award-winning sportswriter for the *Detroit Free Press*. Mick had sought me out to say that he'd heard "a lot of noise [to the effect] that Agase wants you gone." Shortly thereafter, a newspaper headline authenticated the inevitable: SCOTT CAN BE OUT AT EMU. So I was not surprised when I finally got the ziggy from Agase. In fact, I was relieved.

I was replaced by Jim Boyce, a good guy and longtime buddy, who was my tennis partner. Happily, Jim went on to coach EMU to their first winning season since moving up to Division 1.

The Christmas incident at EMU raises an issue that's being hotly discussed today: Should college athletes get paid?

To my mind, these kids absolutely should get paid if their talents help to produce a revenue stream for the school. Many Top Twenty college football and basketball teams generate millions of dollars, yet it's forbidden to buy a hungry kid a hamburger. This makes no sense.

Critics of the pay proposal say that the benefit the "student-athlete" receives is the value of his education. But how many of these kids who accept athletic scholarships from bigtime programs go there to get a college education? What the kids are really there for is to provide entertainment in the form of winning games, track meets, or whatever the specific competition. The more and better he/she entertains, the more money the school makes.

Also, what happens when an athlete finishes his/her athletic eligibility and still hasn't qualified for a diploma? Unfortunately, this is more the norm than the exception. So the kid has been instrumental in generating money for a school and if he/she isn't good enough to turn pro, it's all been for nothing.

This whole situation is just another example of the rampant hypocrisy in college sports.

Then where should this money to pay student-athletes come from?

The top draws at EMU were DePaul and Indiana State when Larry Bird played there. We did have a home-and-home series with Indiana State. At Terre Haute, Bird played with reckless abandon, scored 40-something, and they stomped a mud hole in us. When he played at EMU, his back was hurting, forcing him to play with a kind of cautious efficiency, but even then he still got 30 and pounded us again.

For these games, we'd draw SRO crowds of about 3,000. Normally, against teams like Central Michigan and Western

Michigan, we'd get about 1,500. All the other schools in our conference played in field houses, where the stands were rolled out from the walls, so they likewise had limited capacities. Clearly, then, whatever revenue these colleges generate with their basketball programs is insufficient to pay any meaningful amount of money to their players.

Moreover, the multi-million dollar revenue created by the basketball and football teams of powerhouse programs like Michigan and Michigan State goes to support all the other varsity sports, which create little or no revenue, such as wrestling, gymnastics, track and field, tennis, swimming, fencing, golf, and so on.

My suggestion is that the money for the players should come from the top of the pyramid, namely, the NCAA. There are many NCAA executives making upward of four million dollars every year. And there's no telling how many millions the NCAA reaps from televised college games, especially bowl games and March Madness.

There has recently been public discussion about this issue. As of this writing, the plan is still in its early stages. It tentatively includes lodging, books, and personal computers. Players would also get paid if their personal image is used for advertising purposes. However, nothing is contemplated as far as paying them to play per se. I'll leave the final logistics to others, but this last consideration seems to me to be the obvious *first* step to remedy the blatant exploitation that's endemic in college sports programs.

Looking back on my time at EMU, I've come to understand that although I was a good NBA coach, I was unprepared in many ways to be a successful college coach.

Here are some of the differences in coaching at the two levels:

In the NBA, off-the court encounters between coaches and players seldom occur. After practices and games, the players would zip away and I wouldn't see them again until the next practice or the next game. Even on road trips, the coaches sit in the front in the buses or the planes while the players sit behind them reading, sleeping, listening to music on headphones, or playing cards.

The NBA is in the entertainment business, period. And since nothing is more entertaining to hometown fans than winning, that becomes a pro coach's main objective. That's why he almost always coaches to talent and hardly ever gets into the personal lives of his players.

By contrast, a college coach gets to see his players several times each day. In the cafeteria. Walking around the campus. Coming to his office to ask advice about something. So it's necessary for a college coach to understand his players' backgrounds. What motivates them? A kick in the pants? Or a pat on the back?

A collegiate head coach should be like a father to his players, unafraid to get mad when they mess up, because then they'd be cheating themselves out of being the best they can be. They're kids, after all, so they sometimes repeat the same mistakes fifteen times, which means that a coach has to yell at them fifteen times. When it's necessary, you just do it. But then you have to follow up by helping them correct their mistakes.

If a player reacts to getting yelled at by threatening to quit the team, then it's a college coach's responsibility to teach him how to respond better: "Okay. But what'll quitting get you? If you quit now, you'll do the same thing throughout your life whenever you're faced with some situation that you don't like and that's out of your control. It's up to you. Instead of quitting, learn how to make adjustments." Even if the kid shows some hesitation, tell him you'll see him at the next practice to teach him how to correct his errors.

Throughout my tenure coaching at EMU, I drilled my players on fundamentals, of course, and went to lots of coaching clinics. But I never fulfilled my primary responsibility to them: having enough of a meaningful personal impact. I can see that I should have been more demanding. I lacked the necessary fire to show my full commitment to the players. They want to know that their coach is totally invested in them. And if I didn't seem committed, why should they commit to me?

There were several other reasons why I didn't succeed at coaching at EMU. My inflated ego from my success in the NBA led me to think that I could count on my personal prestige to recruit top-flight players like Magic, Bob Elliott, and Walker D. Russell—something I never had any business doing. Other longtime college coaches—guys like Bobby Knight, Jud Heathcote, and Johnny Orr—had earned their status. I was at fault for not sufficiently respecting my predecessors.

I got the EMU job in April, just a month after I was fired from the Pistons, so I still had an NBA mindset. I failed to realize that to be a successful collegiate coach requires a vastly different set of skills and attitudes than it does to succeed in the NBA. For instance, I had no idea how to set up a process for scouting and recruiting players, nor how to program a suitable practice session. With a 40-minute game that had no shot clock, the games seemed to be over in a flash. I'd been trained to be an NBA coach by playing for Dickie McGuire, Al Bianchi, Gene Shue, and Earl Lloyd. But I simply had no training for my new job.

What would have helped was if I'd served first as an assistant to a college coach, someone I could respect, but as a former NBA Coach of the Year, this was an unlikely scenario. What I should have done was to hire an experienced assistant. Instead, I just went pure basketball.

Looking back, I think that maybe these were the reasons. And they may be more widespread than I think; after all, I wasn't the only ex-NBA player and coach who didn't succeed at coaching at the college level. The only option for anybody (not only coaches) who has messed up at some time and some place—which includes all of us—is to admit one's mistakes and then try to rectify them. This is a task that I've been working on, and will keep working on, for the rest of my ways and days.

Before Agase finally fired me, our total record for the 1977–78 and 1978–79 seasons was 20–34, and showed some slight improvement over my 9–18 rookie season at EMU. The reason Agase gave was as vague as it was standard operating procedure (SOP): I didn't support the athletic program as well as I should have. He failed to say precisely what I might have done to satisfy him.

Whatever. More than anything, as I say, I felt relieved.

And despite being publicly humiliated by the resulting media coverage, I stood and took the bullet like a man. And I'm still standing.

Despite all the problems I had at EMU, I experienced several noteworthy events during my three seasons there:

I volunteered my services to help Senator Don Riegle's (D-MI) successful campaign to get reelected. As I'd done with Hubert Humphrey's campaign for the presidency back in 1968, I was in Mr. Riegle's hand-shaking entourage (along with Detroit Lions' stars Mel Farr, Charlie Sanders, and Lem Barney), and I also gave talks to various organizations. It felt good to play an active role in the democratic process once again.

However, the most joyful and life-changing experience that happened during my stay at EMU was meeting Jennifer Ziehm.

CHAPTER TWENTY

AGAINST THE WIND

My true and lasting happiness began in the fall of 1977 before my second season at EMU when I was watching a scrimmage at the Field House. Practice hadn't started yet, but an informal game had been arranged by the players, some of whom were returning members of my team, the other guys getting ready to try out for the team, and a few who were ineligible for some reason. Doing my due diligence, I would try to show up whenever I could.

On this momentous occasion, I was totally unaware of a slim, pretty, blonde woman sitting two rows behind until we both spontaneously gasped in reaction to some outstanding play. That's when we turned toward each other, and she said, "Coach Scott?"

"Yes."

Her name was Jennifer Ziehm, and she explained that she worked in EMU's intramural office coordinating all of the competitions. Another one of her duties was to judge the floor and bar events during intercollegiate gymnastic competitions. I also learned that she privately taught two off-campus gymnastics classes every week. We continued a light-hearted, casual conversation. Besides being beautiful, it was also evident that she was a highly intelligent person. However, for the time being, that was that.

Since the intramural office was just down the hall from my office, over the following few weeks, we'd sometimes pass in the hall and greet each other with friendly small talk. I simply enjoyed conversing with someone who was not directly involved with the basketball program. While walking past the gym one day I happened upon Jennifer practicing a floor-exercise routine. I was impressed by how gifted and graceful she was. I also noticed that she was much stronger than she looked.

Anyway, sometime before school started in early September, my usual routine was to take a week's vacation in some sunny place like Puerto Rico, or Nassau and Paradise Island in the Bahamas. I had friends in all of these locations and loved to fish, play tennis, listen to some great music, eat wonderful meals, but I stayed away from the casinos. Most of all, the general atmosphere of serenity in these sun-blessed spots helped me to prepare for the next basketball season.

Prior to my third season, when I returned from the Bahamas to EMU, Al Sam from the athletic department came up to me saying, "Coach, there was a good-looking woman asking for you the other day. Here. . . . she left you a message."

The "message" was her phone number, but not her address.

I was curious and also drawn to her, so of course I called her. Yet she had her reservations about the possibility of further exploring our thus-far platonic relationship. After all, I was twenty years older, more than a foot and a half taller, a Black man, and I didn't look anything like Sidney Poitier. So I had to make a move.

My inside man, who turned out to be the facilitator, was Phil Ancheril, a good friend of mine. He was EMU's soccer coach and eventually convinced Jennifer to go out with Phil and his girlfriend on a double date for dinner. Phil picked out the restaurant. It was in Southfield, on the twenty-eighth floor, with a rotating feature that displayed astounding views.

We all had a really good time.

Next up, Jennifer invited Phil and me to a luncheon at a townhouse where she lived with her sister, Debby. This also went well.

Both of these get-togethers increased my hopes that Jennifer and I could develop a meaningful relationship. And she clearly responded in kind.

Shortly thereafter I met Jennifer's parents, Duane and Jeannine, who farmed four hundred acres in northern Michigan. They were remarkable people, and whatever discussions we had about race only revealed how receptive they were to me and to African Americans in general. It was remarkable how quickly and how sincerely they embraced, respected, and trusted me.

It was, in fact, my mom who was a little reluctant at first to fully endorse my new relationship. What worried her was the difference in Jennifer's and my ages. But she soon came around. Duane's and Jeannine's heartwarming welcome to me was repeated later on when they met my mom.

Being raised on a farm had certainly shaped Jennifer's character. In the city, she always looked both ways before crossing a street and had never ridden a subway. As for me, the only grass I ever saw was in a park. She wasn't afraid of hard work; honesty was her only policy; and she was accepting of things that farmers couldn't control. Like the weather. And basketball games. Actually, she had a surprising knowledge of the game, and could talk with some familiarity about Magic, Bird, and my team.

So we started dating on a regular basis.

Jennifer wound up coming to every home game during my last season at EMU, and a miserable season it was. I was mentally wiped out and losing weight. The one thing that nagged me was my not having convinced one special player to transfer to EMU and play in his hometown. That guy was Fred Cofield. Not only was he an extraordinary player (he spent a year with the Knicks), but Fred was a natural leader with a magnetic personality who could single-handedly unify a team.

The year after I was done at EMU, Fred transferred there from Oregon and led the team to the kind of success I had never achieved. I still say jokingly that if Fred had come to EMU while I was there, I'd still be connected with the program.

When Jennifer and I were out in public together, we were often met with stares and the stink eye. Yet I was 6′9″ and 275 pounds, so we never faced any overt hostility.

I was always a Black male, which in America was usually viewed pejoratively. Jennifer, on the other hand, was only white when she was with me.

There was one particular public encounter that made us feel overjoyed: We were having breakfast in a restaurant when a white couple was staring at us. It wasn't obtrusive, yet we couldn't help noticing what they were doing. I was ready to be angry, but this was something Jennifer wouldn't tolerate.

After we were finished eating, the woman came over and apologized for staring. "You're the first interracial couple I've ever seen," she continued, "and I could see by the way you were with each other that you two are the personification of love."

When the woman left, Jennifer had a twinkle in her eyes, saying, "The world is becoming a better place."

This incident was extremely important to us, demonstrating that we were together for all the right reasons.

There was another scene, a private one, that also showed how much we loved each other:

After leaving EMU, I was still searching for employment, so money was tight. One night, when Jennifer was working late and wouldn't get home until eight or even nine, I decided to have a hot meal waiting for her. I had flowers on the table, napkins neatly folded, the plates and silverware beautifully set out. The food itself was limited by the scarcity of our finances, so the main course was Campbell's Chunky Beef Soup over Minute Rice.

I was embarrassed when Jennifer sat down and recognized the food. "It's delicious," she said after taking her first bite. Her loving reaction made my heart melt.

Later, when I started working for Colonial Life & Accident and had some money in the till, I surprised Jennifer by buying her a car when hers broke down and had to be sold for parts.

Looking back, Jennifer said that she treasured that Chunky Soup and rice meal much more than the car. Indeed, it remains one of her favorite stories.

Early in our relationship there was another incident that was very meaningful. I was still trying to find a job and Jennifer was still teaching when, one night, I put all the money I had on the table. "This is it," I said. Jennifer's response was to say, "No," and she put her paycheck on the table.

By doing that, Jennifer emphasized the fact that our coming together was a true partnership.

And the blessings have never stopped.

I had been married twice before, but neither relationship worked out, and both ended in divorce. These experiences made me think of myself as an avowed bachelor. But I couldn't resist Jennifer. We were married on June 27, 1981, and, as they say, the third time was the charm.

Okay. So there I was, forty-two years old, with four children of divorce—John, Karen, David, and Debra. And I love them all. After getting fired from EMU, I was at the end of my professional basketball career, so for the first time in nineteen years, I wasn't protected by its circumscribed world and was now in the cultural mainstream. I had to stand in line just like everybody else. I was just another guy looking for some kind of gig that might turn into a satisfying career.

Getting used to this new life took some doing, mainly because anyone who's been continuously and totally involved with basketball since he was a kid tends to experience an extended adolescence. At the same time, I'm still thankful every day that Jennifer was mature beyond her years and that she always had/ has my back. She helped me to understand and access psychological, emotional, and spiritual depths that were always within me but that I had never realized were there.

Of course, it takes two to tango, yet I'd need to write another book to describe all the ways that Jennifer helped me to become the best (and happiest) person I was capable of becoming. We supported each other emotionally and, when necessary, financially. (Money issues are often the primary reason why marriages have problems.)

There are certain obstacles in life that only Black people in America face, and they do so on a daily basis. The main one is the color of our skin. I had surmounted some and had been stymied by others. Yet the most important feeling that Jennifer nurtured in me was the sense that I was still able to run against the wind.

During my last season at EMU, when I knew it would be my last dance, I'd started looking for some other meaningful employment. This meant that there were some jobs that I swore I'd never take: tending bar, managing a restaurant, selling cars. Selling insurance.

God laughed again.

I was asked to apply for a couple of NBA assistant coaches' jobs, but I didn't want to leave Jennifer or the Ziehms, who had become just as close as my own family. Jennifer now had a position as an ophthalmic technician with the University of Michigan Medical Center, and when she was offered a better job by a company in Texas, she turned it down for similar reasons.

(I should mention that, over the years, Jennifer was promoted to several more responsible spots there. From a lead technician supervising thirty-two people, to a manager supervising seventy-two people, then to an operations manager, where she supervised one hundred ophthalmic practitioners. For sure, she was and is an incredibly gifted person in many fields.)

Mark Andrews was a 4'7" "little person" whom I got to know when he did the game announcements for the Pistons, and we'd become good friends. Despite his diminutive size, Mark had a big, booming voice and perfect diction, so he was eventually hired to do play-by-play announcing for the televised games of the University of Detroit basketball team.

I considered Mark my hero because he took me off the scrap heap and got me back in the public eye. He did this by arranging for me to join him from 1980 to 1982, first on WOMC, the most popular radio station in metropolitan Detroit, and then on TV broadcasts.

One evening we sat down and had a quiet talk. "Being my size," Mark said, "I've gone through a lot in my life. But I never realized what you've also gone through being such a walking overstatement. I mean, how many times have people asked you, 'How's the weather up there?'"

And indeed, the difference in our sizes regularly made for some amusing incidents. For instance, once, when we were in a hotel elevator together, a woman looked up at me and said, "How tall are you?"

"Four-foot-seven," Mark said. And we all laughed.

We were also godfathers to each other's children, I was the best man at his wedding, and we remained good friends until he passed away much too soon at the age fifty-one.

I really enjoyed doing the color announcing. And although I provided whatever insight I had and could describe the strategies the coaches employed, I never criticized any of the coaches' decisions. I knew better because I'd been in that seat myself.

I was well paid for my radio/TV job commentary, but it was only a per-game job, so it was necessarily seasonal and part-time. Now, for the first time in my life, I found myself scanning the Want Ads. And, to my surprise, I found something that intrigued me. I don't remember it verbatim, but it went something like this:

"If you come and work for us, we'll pay you ASAP for what you sell."

It was a "blind" ad, which meant that it didn't specifically mention what the job or the company was. But I took a chance and applied anyway. The company turned out to be Colonial Life & Accident.

An insurance company!?

Nonetheless, I liked the people, their promises to help me establish a career, and their easy acceptance of a Black man, so when they offered me the job, I accepted. I'm sure that my NBA experience as coach and player influenced their decision.

Now I knew why God had laughed.

Colonial furthered my education by having me take business courses at Purdue and the University of Virginia. At first, I knocked on doors trying to sell policies. I did this for about a year and a half with the support, instruction, and motivation of my director, Nick Ginakes, another of my heroes. When I first started, Nick told me that his goal for me was to eventually derive more income from Colonial Life than I had from pro basketball. So I learned as much as I could and worked hard.

Three years later, I was able to thank Nick for helping me to fulfill the goal he'd set for me.

I had been working for Colonial for a year when I was contacted by Time Life, which owned *Sports Illustrated*. They operated a sports-oriented speakers' bureau and wanted to sign me up. I was tempted until Jennifer said this: "Colonial has delivered on everything they promised you, and you have a real chance to make a career there. So you should stay where you are."

Advice that I thankfully followed.

My big break came when I knocked on the door of Coleman Alexander Young, who was the first Black mayor of Detroit and also a prominent politician on the national scene. For sure, my history with the Pistons encouraged him to open the door to me, and with his help I was eventually able to market our policies to all twenty thousand employees of the city. Likewise, by knocking on another welcoming door, I had the opportunity to approach Dr. Arthur Jefferson, who represented the eighteen thousand members of the Detroit school system. With still another connection, this time with the American Federation of Government Employees, my partner, Bill Hill, and I now earned the right to represent about fifty thousand union members who were either city, state, or federal employees. We were proud and grateful to connect with the unions and the union workers. That's because unionized workers were the bedrock of metropolitan Detroit.

The people Jennifer and I met were a major reason we decided to make our home in Michigan. With General Motors, Ford, and Chrysler still operating at full steam, the entire Detroit area was bustling. Even postal workers, owners of small grocery stores, and certainly union members had a wonderful lifestyle. A middle-class paradise, where having a vacation cabin up north, a boat, and an RV were just about normal. There was no other place we even considered moving to.

Nick soon promoted me to marketing director and then, eventually, to be the first Black man ever named Colonial's regional director, making me responsible for overseeing the entire state of Michigan. Forty-one years later, I'm still with Colonial in executive sales and I'm still connected with some of my most valued friends in the company.

During those years, my brother, Marvin, was a single parent who had a job that kept him working until around midnight. So Jennifer and I volunteered to take care of his children—Marvin Jr. and Nicole—in his absence. That meant picking them up from school, feeding them, and bathing them. Having a nine-

and a seven-year-old around was a lot of fun. This also enabled my mom to visit her grandchildren often.

On the weekends, we took the kids to Jennifer's parents' farm. The kids had a ball just running around, riding tractors, swimming in a pool on the property, and enjoying all the animals.

Another blessing to all of us was that the Ziehms and the Scotts were, and still are, really one big family.

Jennifer and I enjoyed the company of our niece and nephew for five years, until Marvin remarried.

An important component of my life, both during and after my involvement with basketball, has always been a passionate interest in helping others whenever possible.

That's why, in 2000, I first became aligned with the Lutheran Child and Family Services (LCFS). Our task was to provide legal and social aid to needy kids throughout Michigan. Then, fifteen years later, the Obama administration organized a national program whose function was to help immigrants between the ages of eight and eighteen to reunite with their parents. When asked to help them, we readily agreed, and became part of the program. So, in addition to working with local kids, we were also involved with youngsters who were mostly from Nicaragua, Honduras, and Guatemala.

After first being held in Houston, they were now being temporarily housed in one of LCFS's facilities in Bay City, Michigan. My job was to visit with these young people and let them know that we had their back. Lots of these kids were articulate in English and were very intelligent. I was proud to have been chosen to do this.

Unfortunately, the efforts of our organization were sometimes hindered by angry demonstrations. Weapons were flashed and a few members of the clergy cast aside their Christian principles to make inflammatory speeches. So our accomplishments were tainted with disappointment. In any event, all of the kids were successfully reunited with their families.

In addition to having the opportunity to realize even a small part of my personal ideal of helping anybody anywhere at anytime, I've had the honor of shaking hands with Dr. Martin Luther King, and of sharing a hug with Malcolm X. I also had connections with other civil rights heroes.

Back in 1966, I was summering in New York, where high-level outdoor games abounded. I was at a playground court located on One Hundred Thirty-Fifth Street and Fifth Avenue, where the games featured such outstanding players as Happy Hairston, Ralph Bacote, Russ Cunningham, Sylvester Blye, and several Globetrotters including Carl Green. I was standing on the sideline waiting for my "next," and there was another player standing beside me waiting for his turn to play. A slender, 6'3" Black man, he seemed familiar.

"Rap?"

"Yeah," he said.

H. Rap Brown. (He later changed his name to Jamil Abdullah Al-Amin.)

So we launched into a discussion about politics, racism, Vietnam, and the civil rights movement. This was at a time when the young kids from the South were passionately involved in obtaining racial equality, while young kids from the North were just as passionately protesting the war in Vietnam. The two groups had begun working together, which had gradually developed into a cauldron of protest energy throughout the country.

Just talking to him face-to-face increased the already high respect I had for Rap, the man and his work.

He was also a good player. Anybody who showed up at any "Big Yard" could really *play*. So, on and off the court, Rap was a winner.

Throughout the years, I've also had several fleeting contacts with other civil rights heroes whose lives and work had deeply touched me. When Jesse Jackson was in Philly, he would sometimes show up at Baker League games, which, along with games at the Rucker, were popular gathering places in African American culture.

I also had the honor of shaking hands with Dr. Ralph Abernathy and Andrew Young when they presented all the participants with trophies after we'd played in a pair of All-Star charity games that benefited the Student Nonviolent Coordinating Committee. I was able to briefly chat with them and express my support for their incredible work. Just getting to physically touch these men whose words and efforts had so profoundly touched me was thrilling.

Summertime games like these were remarkable because guys like Wilt Chamberlain, Oscar Robertson, Willis Reed, and numerous other luminaries played. Being on the court with them made me play at the very top of my game, especially when teamed with Oscar. Besides his incredible skills and talent, Oscar's timing, vision, and uncanny anticipation made all of his teammates better players. During his NBA career, Oscar greatly maximized the effectiveness of guys like Odie Smith, Bob Boozer, Jerry Lucas, Wayne Embry, Jack Twyman, Arlen Bockhorn, and anyone else who was fortunate enough to count him as a teammate. And in those All-Star games, Oscar did the same for me.

Years after I hung up my sneakers and was fired at EMU, I was surprised to find that my coaching career was not finished.

Jennifer's and my eldest daughter, Allison, attended St. Paul's School, which had a basketball program for its elementary students. When she was ten, she played on the combined fifth-grade/sixth-grade girls' team. Of course, I sat in the stands and watched her play. During one particular game, I happened to be sitting next to another parent whose daughter was playing on Allison's team. His name was Mike Rauch and he told me that several parents in the stands were complaining about the coach of the team. So I said to Mike, "We're not going to just sit up here and listen to complaints about the coach. What we're going to do is to offer to help her."

Before the team's next practice session we approached the coach, Mary Lynn Mefford (to the adults, a.k.a. ML), asking her if she thought our help would be beneficial. "Absolutely," she replied enthusiastically. "Please help." So Mike and I became her assistants.

I remember one special game when we were 1 point down with 10 seconds left. We had possession, so as the team huddled around her, ML described the play the girls were to run. Just to make sure they all understood, ML asked if there were any questions.

One of the girls, Laurie Schulz, eagerly raised her hand.

"Yes?" said ML.

"Mrs. Mefford, those are really pretty earrings. Where did you get them?"

We all laughed. And, of course, we won the game.

We were all volunteers, but it wasn't long before the free time of both Mike and ML was curtailed by increased responsibilities in their work situations. Since I was the only one who could be at all the practices and games, I became the head coach.

I had learned several lessons from my previous coaching positions.

But the most important lesson I had also learned was during my time with Colonial. It is that the situation is always the boss. So I was much more involved with the girls than I had been with my players at Detroit and EMU, coaching them according to their individual needs and helping them to both believe in themselves and respect one another.

Before every practice, I convened a team meeting that we called "Town Hall." That's where we discussed any issues that might have come up, plus letting them decide what color hair ribbons they would all wear for our next game.

During practice sessions, the focus was on fundamentals. More than on any other level of competition, these games were decided by made layups and made free throws. Indeed, 90 percent of outcomes in both college and professional games are determined by a team's performance at the foul line.

I also installed a motion offense that was highly successful. However, I really didn't care much whether we won or lost. Developing the on- and off-court confidence of these girls was my paramount interest.

Eventually, I also coached the combined seventh-grade/eighth-grade team and, overall, I continued on the "job" for five years. A special incentive was the opportunity to coach two more of my daughters.

Now, y'all will have to excuse me while a proud father has the chance to brag about these three wonderful young ladies.

When Allison was born, Jennifer and I agreed on her first name (which was derived from an Old German word meaning "noble"), but there was some discussion about what her middle name should be. Jennifer wanted her to be named

"Ray" after me because she believed that Allison would be our only child.

For a girl? The nurse suggested two more appropriate spellings—Rae and Raye. But Jennifer would not be moved.

Okay. Jennifer had just gone through an eighteen-hour labor that included her being cut open by a Cesarean delivery. So if she'd wanted Allison's middle name to be "Harpo," there was no way I would refuse.

By the time Allison was in the sixth grade, it became obvious that she was a terrific athlete, outstanding in basketball, the long jump, the high jump, the quarter-mile run, as well as the hundred-yard dash. She grew to 5'10", and while she was still only in the ninth grade, Valparaiso University offered her a basketball scholarship. However, with the help of some financial aid, she eventually went to her school of choice, Michigan State.

She married Donavon Murdock, who quickly became Jennifer's and my unofficial son. They live only ten minutes from us, so we get plenty of playtime with Miles Ray, our grandson.

Our second daughter, Devon Marie, is named after the Gaelic word meaning "poet," and after my irrepressible Aunt Marie. At 5'9", Devon played the center position for me with a terrific combination of talent and savvy.

Devon isn't married and lives with her boyfriend, but still calls where she grew up "home." She loves kids and is happy being a professional nanny.

Nia is our youngest and her name comes from the Swahili for "brilliance and purpose." At 5'11", Nia is the tallest of the girls, but didn't play basketball when I was coaching the girls' teams. The sports in which she excelled were soccer and cross-country. Having graduated from the University of Michigan (UM), Nia is following in her mother's footsteps, working at

UM as an ophthalmic technician. However, her extraordinary creativity has her thinking about creating a handmade jewelry line. Currently engaged, by the time this book is published, Nia will be married to Mitchell Cassell, another unofficial son of the Scott family.

Maria is the daughter who, like her sisters, is always bright and cheerful. She is now a loving mother and grandmother.

Haley Baker, Nia's best friend since the fourth grade, has become our unofficial adopted daughter.

Of course we love everybody who has been born into our family. We also love everybody who has been gifted to our family.

Raising and coaching my girls was one of the most enjoyable experiences I ever had in my life. A total blessing.

When I was offered another coaching opportunity, I considered it another blessing.

Sometime in the midnineties, I received a call from Eddie, the son of my buddy Mark Andrews. Eddie is my godson and we've stayed in close touch since his father's passing in 2004 when Eddie was still in high school. Like his dad, Eddie is a "little person." An elegant dresser and an incredible athlete, he's really handsome and looks like a smaller Marlon Brando.

"Uncle Ray," he said, "a team I'm on is scheduled to play in a tournament at Wayne State, and we need some coaching."

"It'll be my pleasure."

Officially called the Little People's Tournament, the games were played using the women's smaller ball but with regulation 10-foot baskets. It was an open tournament with no age limit, and all those little guys could really play and were tough enough. The Gold Medal team was incredibly good, so we were thrilled to win the Bronze.

I was pleased to learn there were Olympic Games for Little People and that the participants were also engaged in well-played competitions in soccer, hockey, baseball, as well as every other pastime that we so-called normal people do.

As proud as I was of this last team I ever coached, I was even more proud of how successful Eddie went on to be. After graduating from college, he worked for the NHL's Tampa Bay Rays. Over the years, he also worked in the front offices of the New York Yankees, Sacramento Kings, and the LA Clippers. Moreover, his sister, Hollis, is also a little person who has made her mark as an actress, appearing in the TV series *K.C. Undercover* as well as in the movie *Oz the Great and Powerful*.

I'm still in contact with Eddie and Hollis and so, too, are my daughters. In fact, the Andrews-Scott blended family remains as close as the Ziehms-Scott family.

Blessings abound for all of us.

Whatever my path has been, the vicissitudes of life challenge all of us, so it helps to keep a positive attitude, as does maintaining whatever faith is available to us as individuals.

DRIBBLE ON!

CHAPTER TWENTY-ONE

THE NBA THEN AND NOW

There's one particular game that I do want to forget, but the best I can do is confine it to a hazy memory. This was the situation: A team that will not be named in order to protect the guilty had the ball, down by 2 points, and with five seconds left in the game. Since they also had the terrific advantage of being on a 3-on-1 fast break, being able to tie the game with a layup and go into overtime seemed to be a cinch. However, the two wings ran to the sideline 3-point line and stopped there. Meanwhile the ball handler pulled up and launched a 3-pointer. A win-or-lose shot. Which he missed.

This play was the epitome of what NBA action has come to. Call me an old-timer, but it's a far cry from what the game was like in my early years in the league.

As a rookie in the 1961–62 season, I had been drafted from the Eastern League and had played only one season of college ball, whereas virtually every other player in the NBA had been a celebrated All-American (some notable exceptions were Mike Farmer and Jim Loscutoff, who were strictly role players) and had the benefit of four years' high-quality coaching and competition against other outstanding college players. As a result of their basketball education, just about all of my new peers were mature players.

This meant they had mastered the basic fundamentals of the game. Therefore, at twenty-one or twenty-two, they were well versed in the various arts of cutting, setting and using screens and picks, knowing when backdoor cuts were appropriate, boxing out in the battle for rebounds, fighting their way over screens, passing and shooting techniques, knowing where open shot opportunities would be, knowing how to run fast breaks, making convincing fakes, and proper footwork, and balance. In making a move or attacking the basket, players rarely dribbled more than three times, kept their dribbles totally protected, and no team ran isolation plays. Plus, except for those who had exclusively played zones in college, they knew how to play defense.

In addition, players who had full exposure to college coaching were raised in systems, so they welcomed 5-on-5 game plans, along with the sacrifices and disciplines involved. And let's not discount the enormous publicity All-American players received. For the most part, televised college games were only available in New York City, so basketball fans in the rest of the country were kept up-to-date on their favorite teams and players by reading newspapers or popular magazines like *Sport, Sports Illustrated, Sporting News,* and most importantly, *Street & Smith's,* which forecast each forthcoming season's All-Americans and highlighted all the other outstanding players. And basketball fans everywhere listened to radio broadcasts. This meant that outstanding college players already had significant followings among the basketball public. Newspapers were of particular interest because they printed box scores, which enabled fans to find out how their favorite player had played, even if the player wasn't the game's top scorer, rebounder, or passer.

The exaltation of the best college players by the media and by the public relations departments of their schools also determined the draft selections made by many teams. This process began with the subjective boosting of football candidates for the Heisman Trophy, and college basketball programs soon followed suit. For example, when the Knicks drafted Richie Guerin, he was familiar to New York fans. Similarly, Philadelphia pleased its fans by drafting homegrown talent like Tom Gola, Ernie Beck, Guy Rodgers, Paul Arizin, Larry Hennessy, and, through the territorial draft, Wilt Chamberlain.

From the midfifties to the midsixties, another indication of how the ground was shifting in America was that many Black players from major college programs that had previously been all-white became formidable NBA players: Don Barksdale (UCLA), Maurice Stokes (St. Francis, PA), Dick Ricketts (Duquesne), Bob Boozer (Kansas), Tom Hawkins (Notre Dame), Joe Caldwell (Arizona), Lucius Allen (UCLA), Jim Barnes (University of Texas at El Paso), Tom Thacker (Cincinnati), Bill Bridges (Kansas), Cazzie Russell (Michigan), Dave Bing (Syracuse), Wayne Hightower (Kansas), Walt Hazzard (UCLA), George Wilson (Cincinnati), Hubie White (Villanova), Billy McGill (Utah), Tom Stith (St. Bonaventure), Walter Dukes (Seton Hall), Chet Walker (Bradley), Willie Jones (Northwestern), Leroy Ellis (St. John's), Ed Fleming (Niagara), Ray Felix (LIU), Gene Wiley (Wichita State), Joe Roberts (Ohio State), Guy Rodgers (Temple), Jackie Moore (La Salle), Elgin Baylor (Seattle), Al Butler (Niagara), plus several of the Johnsons and Joneses (who, if they were all listed, would require another chapter).

Ben Warley (1962–67) and Joe Buckhalter (1961–63) both hailed from Tennessee State, Cleveland Buckner (1961–63) from Jackson State, and Bob Hopkins (1956–62) from Grambling were the early players from HBCU schools. So, too, was Dick Barnett (Tennessee A&I), a dynamic scorer and underrated defender who had a long, illustrious career (1959–74) that featured making significant contributions to the Knicks' championship in 1970. And remember that Earl Lloyd (1950–60) out of West Virginia State was the first.

From the time I started playing basketball until now, I've always been a fan of these guys, individually and collectively.

Inclusion was becoming more popular in American culture, and the NBA was in the forefront of this movement.

For example:

Colin Kaepernick was an accomplished quarterback who led the San Francisco 49ers to the NFL's championship game in 2013. Throughout the 2016 season, however, Kaepernick chose to protest the racial injustice, police brutality, and systemic oppression in America by kneeling during the pregame playing of the national anthem. As a result, he was blackballed by every club in the league.

Compare this to what happened to Chris Jackson, a high-scoring guard for the Denver Nuggets (averaging as much as 19.4 points in each of two seasons), who converted to Sunni Islam in 1991. Two years later, he changed his name to Mahmoud Abdul-Rauf. Obedient to the laws set down in the Koran, Abdul-Rauf was forbidden to take part in any ceremony that honored nationalism, oppression, or tyranny. As a Black man, he believed that the national anthem fulfilled all of these definitions, so he sat during the playing of our national anthem, and when he did, he was suspended. His banishment lasted only one game, after which Mahmoud took to staying in the locker room while "The Star-Bangled Banner" was played. Then, after consulting with Kareem Abdul-Jabbar, Mahmoud stood with his teammates, bowed his head, and softly said an Islamic prayer.

Subsequently, Abdul-Rauf played another seven years for Denver. Then, after playing in Turkey during the NBA's 1999–2000 season, he was signed by the Vancouver Grizzlies for the following season.

Notice the difference between how America's most popular sport, professional football, dealt with Kaepernick, who was punished by being banished from the league and how the NBA treated Abdul-Rauf. In the NBA a way was found for Abdul-Rauf to act in accordance with his beliefs and still continue to play.

Unfortunately, Mahmoud's courageous stand for religious freedom didn't spare him from private tragedy. In 2001, he contracted to have a house built in his hometown of Gulfport, Mississippi. When "KKK" was painted on the construction site, Abdul-Rauf was reluctant to occupy the house when the work was completed, so he put it up for sale. Shortly thereafter, the house burned to the ground, a deed that the local police decided was arson.

I would be remiss if I failed to fully honor the neglected and all-but-forgotten greatness of several Black players who played in the NBA during the 1950s.

The following five players from Duquesne were a special group:

Dick Ricketts was employed by the Rochester Royals mostly as a role player (1955–58), but was in fact an accomplished scorer, rebounder, and passer. He also had movie-star looks.

Jim Tucker was a man of character and great carriage, who played with the Syracuse Nationals from 1954 to 1957. An accomplished jump shooter, he understood all the ins and outs of the game.

At 6'3" and 200 pounds, Sihugo Green (1956–67) played for six NBA teams, was incredibly strong, and played like a smaller version of Charles Barkley.

Fletcher Henderson never considered playing in the NBA, went to med school instead, and became a celebrated heart surgeon.

The fifth starter was a talented Jewish playmaker named Mickey Winograd, who also failed to play in the NBA.

What made these Iron Dukes (so-called because these five routinely played 40 minutes per game) noteworthy was that coach Dudey Moore put four African Americans on the floor to start a game, a radical move for a non-HBCU school in 1954. And these guys could play, finishing the season at 26–3 and reaching the championship game at the prestigious NIT before losing to a powerful Holy Cross team led by Togo Palazzi and Tom Heinsohn.

Before a brain injury prematurely terminated his career (1955–58), Maurice Stokes was unquestionably one of the greatest players in the history of the league. Yet he is mostly remembered for being the subject of a biographical film, *Maurie*, and also for the Mo Stokes All-Star Games that were played at Kutsher's for many years to raise money for his medical expenses.

Chuck Cooper (1950–56) and my mentor, Earl Lloyd (1950–59), were both rugged rebounders and savvy defenders.

Hank DeZonie was an ex-Globie and ace rebounder, who played six games for the Tri-Cities Blackhawks at the beginning of the 1950–51 season. Disgusted with the racial discrimination he faced, DeZonie quit the team and the league.

After starring at LIU, the lean and handsome 6'11" Ray Felix went on to play for several NBA teams (1953–61). He was the first African

American to be chosen Rookie of the Year based on his output of 17.6 points and 13.3 per-game rebounds for the Baltimore Bullets.

Nat "Sweetwater" Clifton's contract was sold to the Knicks by the Globetrotters. From 1950 to 1957, he was the best non-center defender in the NBA.

Bob Hopkins's four-year career (1956–60) with Syracuse was curtailed by a severe ankle injury. When he was healthy, Hopkins was an effective scorer and rebounder with extraordinary elevation. For a brief period in 1977, Hopkins succeeded his uncle, Bill Russell, as coach of the SuperSonics before being replaced by Lenny Wilkens.

Davage "Dave" Minor (1951–53) was a scrappy, speedy guard from UCLA, who played for Baltimore and Milwaukee.

Ben Swain (1958–59) from Texas Southern was another early HBCU player who made it into the NBA. While he had an effective post-up game during his time with the Celtics, his offense was limited because he lacked a midrange jumper.

Even before Maurice Stokes's grand entry into the NBA, Don Barksdale was universally considered to be one of the best players in the league. He graduated from UCLA in 1947, becoming the first African American to be a consensus All-American. His next honor was being chosen, in 1948, as the first Black man on a basketball team that represented America in the Olympic Games. This was the result of persistent lobbying by Fred Maggiora, a member of the Olympic Committee and local politician, to overcome the fierce resistance of many of his fellow committee members.

Despite Barksdale's resume, he wasn't eligible for the NBA Draft until 1951. Until then, he served a stint in the army, then played with an Oakland-based AAU (Amateur Athletic Union) team. Barksdale was twenty-eight when he entered the NBA, and despite his belief that his best years were behind him, his incredible moves and star-touching hops earned him another milestone when, in 1953, he became the first African American to play in an NBA All-Star game. This honor was even more significant since, at the time, inclusion in the game was voted on by the NBA players. His NBA career was shortened (1951–55) due to injuries.

Unfortunately, Maurice Stokes and Don Barksdale are among the most neglected all-time great players in NBA history.

The vast majority of white fans never heard of the best players in the HBCU conferences. Thankfully, Earl Lloyd, Red Holzman, and Red Auerbach were more interested in scouting and signing talent than in any other considerations. Also, even though Haskell Cohen was an NBA administrator, he had significant influence on the scouting of African American players.

Also, when Joe Lapchick was one of the Original Celtics (a great touring team of the 1930s), he pleaded with his teammates to add some African American players from the Harlem Renaissance, an all-Black touring team similar to the Globetrotters, but was turned down. Later, when Lapchick first coached at St. John's and then the Knicks, he welcomed Black players to his teams.

A special mention must be made of Marty Blake. When he worked for the Hawks, he was primarily responsible for drafting Cleo Hill, Bill Bridges, Zelmo Beaty, Fred LaCour, Chico Vaughn, and John Barnhill, and later Paul Silas, even though St. Louis was then well-known as being a segregated city.

When I was a rookie, the most prominent players were white: Dolph Schayes (Syracuse); Richie Guerin (New York); Bob Cousy, Tom Heinsohn, and Frank Ramsey (Boston); Bob Pettit and Cliff Hagan (St. Louis); Gene Shue and Bailey

Howell (Detroit); Jerry West (Los Angeles); Paul Arizin (Philadelphia); and Jack Twyman (Cincinnati).

At that time, there were only four Black players who were considered to be stars: Elgin Baylor, Oscar Robertson, Bill Russell, and Wilt Chamberlain, whose entries into the NBA preceded mine by several years. Lenny Wilkens would have been an addition to this fabulous foursome had he not been serving in the military.

So there I was—a rookie routinely getting my lunch eaten by experienced, well-educated guys like Dolph Schayes, Tom Heinsohn, Willie Naulls, Paul Arizin, Bob Boozer, Bob Pettit, and Elgin Baylor. For example, if I turned my head to peek at the ball just for an instant—*Woosh!* These guys made backdoor cuts and wound up with easy baskets. Us young guys were also subject to strategic elbows, the casual body-bump, the surreptitious hand on the back or on the hip.

These veterans would also set traps to catch rookies. For example, knowing when and how we would pivot to take a jumper, an opponent would beat us to the spot at just the right time and steal the ball. Likewise, teams would force the ball into areas where their shot-blockers held sway.

However, there were some guys whose lunch I ate, and that's why I lasted so long.

Remember, I was (and still am) the only player drafted directly from the Eastern League, so I had a significant advantage over players who'd been drafted straight from college. I had competed on mostly equal terms against all those great players in the Eastern League like Bill Spivey, Roman Turman, Jack Molinas, Sherman White, and the rest. I had played the pro game for more than two seasons, which eased my transition to the NBA to a certain degree.

Still, the size, talent, and experience of my new opponents did make a difference.

For one thing, with so many great big men in the NBA controlling the basket area, offensive rebounds were as rare as the proverbial hen's teeth.

Here's something else that NBA newbies like me had (and still have) to learn: how to fulfill the adjustments that coaches make during time-outs, quarter-breaks, and especially during the halftime intermissions. This last requirement is especially vital, because the two most critical periods of any game are the initial 5 minutes of the third quarter, where teams have an extended opportunity to make adjustments; and the last 5 minutes of the game, when teams have to implement adjustments made in time-outs. I call them "the deadly minutes."

The increased power, speed, and quickness of the NBA game were other new factors I had to deal with. Basically, in addition to everything else, the NBA was a strong-man's league. How, then, could I use my own abilities to cope? Because if I couldn't cope, then I wouldn't survive.

The dominant forces in the NBA at the time were the big men: Russ, Wilt, Willis, Bells, Kareem, Nate Thurmond, Walter Dukes, Johnny Kerr, Clyde Lovellette, and others. If the ball went to Wilt, Kareem, Nate, Bells, Willis, and Lovellette it usually stayed there. Johnny Kerr was one of the few bigs who looked to pass before shooting.

The upshot was that guards and forwards didn't have much room to drive. So they, and even forwards (like me), had to be able to score from outside. Setting aside the close-in dominance of the center, the NBA was also a jump shooter's league by necessity. Yet, if those designated shooters only made 40 to 42 percent of their shots, their teams would be in for a long night.

I was extremely fortunate to be drafted by the Pistons, where Earl Lloyd, Dickie McGuire, Walter Dukes, as well as my roommate, Willie Jones, all took a special interest in helping me learn the NBA game. And it was Earl who set the tone. This was unusual, because veteran players are generally totally unwilling to mentor young players who will eventually diminish, then take over, their playing time.

Furthermore, some young players are not receptive to being taught by their elders. Fortunately, I was receptive.

There were several key moments when the game changed: Red Auerbach dismantled the racial quota system, and Magic and Bird turned the NBA into a global commodity.

Another one of these turning points began in the 1975–76 season, when Bill "Poodle" Willoughby and Darryl "Chocolate Thunder" Dawkins graduated directly from high school into the NBA. This meant that they and the others to come had to instantly change from playing in about twenty-five games against other high school players, with each game lasting 32 minutes, to playing a total of one hundred 48-minute preseason, playoff, and regular-season games against professionals, and playing them in three time zones. Understandably, such players had trouble making any kind of adjustments, and too many of them were more interested in establishing their "brand" than in learning the ins and outs of the pro game.

And what about staying/getting in the necessary physical and mental states? Eating the right foods at the right times. Getting enough sleep. Learning new game-preparation routines. Not to mention playing against bigger and more experienced players who have refined their skills. Moreover, how many of these kids had mostly or totally played zones in high school and therefore had no idea how to play man-to-man defense?

With the notable exceptions of LeBron, Jermaine O'Neal, and Lou Williams, these eighteen-year-olds were always a step behind. Sure, some ultimately learn their trade, but even a supremely talented player like Kevin Garnett took years to become a meaningful player. Unfortunately, only some of these too-young men eventually made the grade.

Then there's Darryl Dawkins. If Dawkins had played in a good college program for only two years, he would have been too much for any of his NBA opponents to handle. As it was, for all of the 776 games and thirteen seasons in his pro career, Dawkins was always a high-schooler playing in the NBA. It was unfair to expect Dawkins to avoid being dominated by the likes of Willis Reed, Dave Cowens, Kareem, Bill Walton, and Bob Lanier. Indeed, Dawkins and dozens of others were the same players when they retired as they were when they were rookies.

Kobe Bryant made an initial impact after entering the NBA from Lower Merion High School only because his father, Joe "Jellybean" Bryant went from playing in the NBA to playing in Italy. So during the summer vacations, when he was still a schoolboy, Kobe had the opportunity to compete in a high level of competition against older, experienced Italian and transplanted American players. Even so, Kobe had to wait his turn for the chance to become a dominant force in the NBA.

It seemed to me that the admission of high school players, regardless of their talents, brought about a loss of interest by fans in the NBA.

Another significant alteration came in the 1976–77 season when the Denver Nuggets, Indiana Pacers, San Antonio Spurs, and New Jersey Nets joined the NBA. These refugees from the ABA brought with them several features of the now-defunct league: flying dunks, spread offenses, dancing girls at every stoppage of the clock, and most important and most devastating, the 3-point shot. In other words, everything but the striped ball.

Furthermore, there were now new incredible talents being absorbed into the NBA from the ABA, players such as George Gervin, Julius Erving, Dan Issel, David Thompson, Connie Hawkins, and the return of Rick Barry. However, the likes of Elvin Hayes, Wes Unseld, Jack Sikma, Hakeem Olajuwon, Patrick Ewing, Moses Malone, Kevin McHale, Robert Parish, Kareem, Lanier, Dave Cowens, Bill Walton, and James Donaldson were still roaming the lane, so the big men remained the NBA's most forceful players. With the exceptions of Artis Gilmore, Zelmo Beaty, and Billy "The Whopper" Paultz, there was such a lack of dominant centers in the ABA that the newcomers into the NBA were compelled to learn how to play with big men.

However, it should be noted that a certain precursor to the ABA-to-NBA transition was perhaps the one player with the most lasting influence on the established league. This was Charlie Scott, who moved from the Virginia Squires to the Phoenix Suns at the tail end of the 1971–72 NBA season. Charlie was a 6'6" point guard who could shoot, leap, run, and make good decisions. He represented the advent of the tall point guards that culminated (thus far) in the supersized Magic Johnson.

The biggest change in the NBA game was due to the decline of Magic and Bird, which led David Stern to look for a new player to be highlighted by the league's marketing machine. It was genius on the part of Stern that, after the Bulls ended the Pistons' championship reign, he picked Michael Jordan. At the same time, Nike was engaged in a similar search to advertise its product and also selected MJ. After all, in addition to being a winner, Michael's spectacular play was entertaining. Another facet of Stern's genius was allowing Nike to make Jordan and Spike Lee the first Black men to appear on nationally televised commercials. Remember Mars Blackmon and "I Like Mike"? This meant that Nike was essentially footing the bill for Stern's decision to make Jordan the face of the NBA.

The success of this process led the league, as well as the media at large, to celebrate the achievement of individuals, while neglecting the achievement of teams.

Another dramatic change occurred in 1979 when the league adopted the 3-point shot. However, the extra-point shot has a long history that predates the NBA's drawing this particular line:

The debut occurred in 1945 in an intercollegiate game against Columbia and Fordham when the line was set at 21 feet. Another single-game experiment took place in 1958, when the line was moved a foot farther back in a game between St. Francis (NY) and Siena. But nothing came of this radical idea.

Upon its creation in 1961, Abe Saperstein's American Basketball League was the first pro outfit to install the 3-point shot. Six years later, the ABA followed suit. Finally, in 1977, the NBA adopted the 3-point line.

During his tenure coaching the Houston Rockets (2017–20), Mike D'Antoni's offensive game plan called for getting up as many shots as possible—preferably within 8 seconds of each possession. The idea being that the more shots a team launches, the more points they will score and the more wins they will achieve. As a result, the Rockets were the first NBA team to use 3-point shots as their primary weapon.

Nowadays, that same weapon has become nuclearized.

And to my way of thinking, here's why all this has been done: When marketing the game became the be-all and end-all, the NBA was driven to appeal to the largest audience possible.

Forget about intricate 5-on-5 offenses, back screens, back cuts, high-low plays, and the like. Now, with the simplicity and excitement of 3-point shots and dunks, even non-fans could understand NBA action. And it worked! Since the current game is made for TV, and not necessarily to appeal to the fans in the stands, TV ratings have soared. No surprise that TV networks pay more and more to broadcast NBA contests.

A similar process has afflicted both Major League Baseball (with every batter striving to hit a home run with every swing) and the NFL (with the passing game becoming dominant). And what about the NHL's instituting individual break-away attempts to decide tie games? All of these over-the-top game plans are primarily aimed at marketing and making as much money as possible.

By turning what once were the worst possible shots into glamorous extra-point shots, the NBA has altered the basic metrics and strategies of the game. Low-post play has just about vanished. Since 3-point misses have a propensity to hit the front rim and rebounds usually bounce back to the foul line and beyond, offensive rebounding is a lost art. When these long rebounds are captured by defensive guards or forwards, then freewheeling fast breaks usually result. Today's players are generally quicker, faster, and have greater lift than we had, so instead of the stately stuffs made by Wilt and Russ, an average NBA game today is filled with dramatic flying dunks on the run.

Too often I see a player driving into the paint, getting as close as a foot from the basket, then kicking the ball out to a teammate who's twenty-five feet from the hoop. Seems to me that this move sacrifices an almost sure deuce and/or foul for a high-risk trey. I don't like this transaction. Unless, of course, the 3-ball shooter is Steph Curry, who is probably the greatest long-range shooter in the history of the game.

Throughout his career in regular-season games, Curry has been shooting 43.4 percent from beyond the line, although his accuracy falls to 40.1 percent during the playoffs. As such, Curry sets the bar very high, and every team in the league is looking for any player who can shoot 40.0 percent or more. However, a successful make-rate in the neighborhood of 35 percent is thought to be acceptable.

It's also acceptable for a player who shoots 25 percent from beyond the line to hoist up a 3-ball even when there are double digits left on the shot clock.

Thus the NBA now features a plethora of seven-footers who do a large part of their scoring from "downtown." I can imagine that if Wilt and Kareem were young players today, they'd also have to add 3-point shooting to their respective repertoires. And Shaq for sure.

It should be noted that while Curry is a revolutionary player who heralds the new school, LeBron's all-around game is a wonderful blast from the past.

I'm okay with the wide-open spacing that offenses now employ to facilitate 3-point shooting; however, I object to the advent of the so-called Euro Step. This basically legalizes what used to be called "walking" or "traveling." This bonus step gives penetrators a huge edge. Also, there are some players who catch the ball a step in front of the 3-point line, then, without putting the ball on the floor, do a two-foot shuffle to get into 3-point territory.

For sure, getting a triple-double is always an accomplishment. To get it done requires considerable talent and effort.

Nevertheless, it should also be noted that during the 1961–62 season, Oscar Robertson *averaged* a triple-double consisting of 30.8 points, 11.4 assists, and 12.5 rebounds per game for the Cincinnati Royals. Then in 1963–65, O's per-game output included 31.4 points, 11.0 assists, and 9.9 rebounds. During two other seasons he likewise came within fractional numbers of duplicating his feat.

Looking back, Oscar has said this: "If I had known that getting triple-doubles would become such a big deal, I would have done it every season."

Yet with all of these caveats, I still believe that the pro game has retained its inherent beauty. Veterans like LeBron, Rajon Rondo, and Carmelo Anthony are still good players, and the way that young players have adapted to the new game is a joy for me to watch. As expected, they play with skill and talent, but they also play their hearts out. The NBA's center stage now stars the likes of Trae Young, Damian Lillard, Devin Booker, Luka Dončić, Giannis Antetokounmpo, and several others. The emergence of the new players in the new game is a main reason why the NBA is enjoying a resurgence in popularity.

Still another indication of how much the game has changed is that Denver's Nikola Jokić was named the MVP in 2021. In my view, "The Joker" absolutely deserved the honor, but throughout all the years that I've been connected with and followed the game, I never expected that a European player could/would win that award.

To update Bob Dylan, *the times they are a-changed.*

CHAPTER TWENTY-TWO

WELCOME TO MY AMERICA

I was twelve years old back in 1950 when my uncle drove my brother and me to Washington, DC. That trip marked the first time I experienced the notorious Jim Crow laws. But in the late summer of 1955, I became aware of something that was much worse.

Emmett Till was a fourteen-year-old African American from Chicago who was visiting relatives in Money, Mississippi. This was always a special time for African American families that had been separated during the migration of so many Southern Blacks to Northern cities. The kids were out of school, the crops had been planted, and everyone was looking forward to having a joyous summertime.

But for Emmett and his family the expected joy quickly turned to tragedy when a white woman claimed that the boy had come into the store where she was working, "wolf whistled" at her, and grabbed her around her waist.

Really? A fourteen-year-old Black boy from Chicago touching a white woman in Mississippi?

Yet the woman's charge was taken as gospel.

The result was that Till was kidnapped by a crew of angry white men led by her husband and forced to carry a seventy-five-pound cotton gin fan to the bank of the Tallahatchie River. He was beaten nearly to death, his eyes gouged out, and then shot in the head. His body was then tied to the fan with barbed wire and tossed into the river.

When his mutilated corpse was found several days later, his mother had her dead son brought back to Chicago. The funeral director advised that Emmett's casket be kept closed during the funeral, but his mother insisted on keeping it open, saying, "Let everybody see what they did to my son." His body was swollen to nearly twice its normal size, and his face was so smashed that he could not be recognized.

The news came as a shock to me, and because it went national, to a great many white people as well. The sheer horror of it was truly soul-shaking.

There were two major pictorial magazines, *Look* and *LIFE*, both of which primarily appealed to a white audience. However, there were also two magazines—*EBONY,* a monthly, and *Jet,* a weekly—that provided news that was relevant to our community. It was in the pages of *Jet* that photos of the ghastly remains of Emmett Till were displayed.

I was only two years older than Emmett, so I identified with him. My disgust, fear, and horror were visceral, feelings that persist to this day.

The murderers were arrested but were declared innocent at a phony trial after an all-white jury made a pretense of deliberating for an hour. The attention from most of the national media faded after the trial. Then, in 2017, the woman who had accused Emmett recanted, saying that he had done nothing to insult or even embarrass her.

On June 12, 1963, eight years after Till's murder and while the civil rights movement was on the march, another shocking act emerged out of Mississippi. Medgar Evers, a World War II veteran who had seen action in Normandy, was living in Jackson at the time, employed by the local chapter of the NAACP as a fieldworker. He had already survived the firebombing of his house and having nearly been run down by a car. But Byron De La Beckwith, a member of both the KKK and the White Citizens' Council, finally caught up with him long enough to put a fatal bullet in Evers's back. Two hung juries kept Beckwith out of jail until he was convicted in a 1994 trial, and he eventually died in prison.

Meanwhile, Evers was given a full military funeral in Arlington National Cemetery. But the shock and anger was made even worse by a sense of déjà vu. Again?

Yes, again.

On September 15, 1963, the Sixteenth Street Baptist Church in Birmingham, Alabama, was bombed. Four young African American girls were killed. Say their names: Addie Mae Collins, Cynthia Dionne Wesley, Carole Rosamond Robertson, and Carol Denise McNair. Then came another phony trial.

Yet again.

On November 23, 1963, President Kennedy was assassinated in Dallas. Although there was not a racial component this time, the shock and horror was as widespread among Black communities as it was throughout the country and the world.

Later on, when I was with a group from Colonial attending a meeting in Dallas, we all went on a tour of the Texas School Book Depository. Judging from the angle from there to where the motorcade had passed, it was clear to me that Oswald could never have made that killing shot. If the truth hasn't been revealed almost sixty years later, what does that say about my and everybody's America?

And again!

On June 21, 1964, the bodies of two Jewish kids from New York City were found. Michael Schwerner and Andrew Goodman had left the safety of their home to travel to Neshoba County, Mississippi, to help register Black voters. These courageous young kids were joined by James Chaney, a Black kid from the area, who was equally as brave. Yet, it was barely seven months after JFK's assassination that the bodies of these three dedicated civil rights workers were found buried in an earthen dam just a few miles from the all-Black Mt. Zion United Methodist Church.

Again and again and . . .

Robert Kennedy. Dr. Martin Luther King. Malcolm X. . . .

Viola Liuzzo was a white woman who came to Mississippi from Detroit to work for the Southern Christian Leadership Council. One of her jobs was to drive African Americans to places where they could register to vote. But on March 25, 1965, Liuzzo, the mother of five, was shot and killed by several members of the KKK. Nobody was surprised when, in still another fake trial, all the killers were acquitted.

Viola Liuzzo is still revered in her hometown of Detroit. So much so that in 2020 a neighborhood park on the city's west side was named Viola Liuzzo Park, and a statue of her was erected there.

Despite my privileged position as an NBA/ABA player, I was no less saddened, shocked, and outraged by all these atrocities—but I was not confused, knowing as I did the huge part racism plays in our culture.

Is there any difference in the racial situation in America between my earlier NBA days and now?

The answer is yes, both positive and negative.

On the minus side, bullets have replaced bombs and ropes, and guns are everywhere. My brothers and sisters are still being shot on an almost weekly basis. Kids, both Black and white, are often reluctant to play hoops in playgrounds or schoolyards, simply because a fiercely debated foul call could result in a player with a beef returning to the game with a deadly weapon.

Tragically, there have been too many Black victims of police brutality. Fortunately, however, the circumstances of one particular victim—George Floyd—became an international incident because the crime was videotaped. Derek Chauvin was only brought to justice because a courageous seventeen-year-old bystander, Darnella Frazier, used her cell phone to record the incident. This visible evidence of such a ruthless killing sparked justice-seeking protests, not only throughout America but all over the world.

It's noteworthy that such an unprecedent worldwide reaction shows what the outrage of unbiased citizens can accomplish.

As of this writing, very few murders of African Americans by police have resulted in convictions and jail time. In April 2015, Walter Scott was shot in the back eight times while fleeing a police officer in North Charleston, South Carolina. The cop was eventually tried, convicted, and given a twenty-year sentence. In Dallas, Texas, in September 2018, a policewoman entered an apartment that she'd mistakenly thought was hers and fatally shot the resident, Botham Jean, who had committed no crime nor was suspected of any. Her sentence was ten years.

Most white murderers of Black people, however, escape justice. One glaring example is George Zimmerman, who shot down young innocent Trayvon Martin and not only went free but makes money giving lectures to groups sympathetic to his "Stand Your Ground" defense. He also made money by selling the murder weapon as a souvenir!

In my opinion, the true promise of America has to come from the ground up. Here are some of the changes I view as necessary:

Urban communities have to be made safer through police *reform* that's fair to everyone.

Public playgrounds, parks, and recreation centers have to be modernized in all low-income neighborhoods.

The current and impending disasters of climate change absolutely have to be resolved, because they affect everyone, particularly the poor and disadvantaged.

The health industry should not be allowed to be profit-driven.

The whole education system must be revised. It's absurd and untenable that students graduate from college owing vast sums of money and still can't find suitable jobs.

For all these things to come about, there first needs to be an honest dialogue among all the various cultural and racial groups. And despite the laws that so many states have instituted to make voting more difficult for poor people and people of color, I firmly believe that this up-front communication is not only possible but inevitable. That's because more and more young people are increasingly aware of what needs to happen for their futures to be safe, successful, and enjoyable.

It's axiomatic that racism in general must be addressed. White supremacists firmly believe that African Americans are an inferior race, are descended from people of the bush, and that they still retain many primitive characteristics. They don't know (and don't want to know) anything about the many ancient African civilizations that were in fact highly developed.

For example, there was the Kingdom of Aksum, which was founded around 400 BCE and lasted for 540 years. These people had a written language, minted their own coins, had the engineering know-how to erect hundred-foot towers, and developed terrace farming and irrigation.

Or the Kingdom of Kush, which began in 1070 BCE and lasted for 1,400 years. The Kushites were farmers and warriors, famous for their deadly accuracy with the bow and arrow. They mined iron and gold, made clothing from the cotton they grew, and built pyramids.

Then there was the Empire of Ghana, which encompassed a large area of West Africa from 300 to 1100 CE and is credited with inventing iron tools.

There was the Land of Punt, founded in 2500 CE. And the Mali Empire. And the Songhai Empire. And several more.

I don't understand why it's so difficult for racists to believe that my community has a long-standing loyalty to America. How many hundreds of thousands of Blacks risked their lives to serve in all of America's wars? How many of these suffered crippling wounds? And how many died?

For example, the all-Black Fifty-Fourth Massachusetts Infantry Regiment showed extraordinary bravery while fighting in the Union Army during the Civil War. The division was commanded by Colonel Robert Shaw, a white man—a fact that was apparently considered so repellent to his white superiors that when Shaw died, he was refused burial with military honors and was instead interred with the fallen Black soldiers he had led. Several of Shaw's descendants approved, saying, "That's exactly where he belongs."

The same fighting spirit was exhibited by African American soldiers in World Wars I and II, in Korea, Vietnam, Desert

Storm, and Afghanistan. There is no reason why the patriotism of Black Americans should be called into doubt.

I'm proud that pro basketball has assumed an important place in the fight for equality. And that George Floyd's murder prompted both Black and white NBA players to support the Black Lives Matter movement. During the 2019–20 season, when all the NBA teams were locked in the bubble because of the Covid pandemic, virtually every player took to wearing Black Lives Matter T-shirts when warming up. In addition, several people in leadership positions have also spoken out— for example, coaches Doc Rivers (before he was fired by the Clippers), Gregg Popovich (San Antonio), Steve Kerr (Golden State), and Mark Cuban, owner of the Dallas Mavs.

"BLM" was even printed on the courts in the bubble, and in the 2020–21 season, several NBA teams followed suit when they resumed playing on their home courts. BLM is not a political statement. It's simply a demand for justice.

The NBA's commitment to racial justice was further demonstrated in a significant on-court event. On March 4, 2021, all three referees on the court in the prime-time and highly rated NBA's All-Star game were graduates of HBCU colleges: Tom Washington (Norfolk State), Tony Brown (Clark Atlanta), and Courtney Kirkland (Southern). This amounted to a historic statement by Adam Silver and the NBA's board of governors.

I don't want to forget the WNBA. The league may have an attendance problem, but they feature some of the best women players in the world. Just to name a few: Diana Taurasi, Sabrina Ionescu, Candace Parker, A'ja Wilson, Elena Delle Donne, the 6′9″ Liz Cambage, and 6′9″ Brittney Griner. They play a version of basic basketball that's interesting, entertaining, and well worth watching.

WNBA players, both Black and white, have also shown their support for racial and cultural justice. For example, the Atlanta Dream was owned by Kelly Loeffler, an ultra-conservative who lost her bid to become one of Georgia's senators in the 2020 election. The women on the team so objected to having to play for Loeffler that she was forced to sell the team.

And when Kentucky's attorney general, in the official press conference to discuss the recent murder of Breonna Taylor, didn't even identify her, WNBA players quickly responded by wearing T-shirts that simply read, "Say Her Name." What the attorney general did say was that the policeman who killed her had had "a bad day."

In so many ways, the NBA and the WNBA are showing the way for a future in which all Americans have a seat at the table.

And here's, perhaps, the one most important thing that too many people fail to understand: The vast majority of Black Americans approach their fair-minded fellow citizens with open hands offering love and respect.

However, just offering love and respect means nothing if some people aren't willing to receive them. When, someday, this gift is accepted with goodwill, then that, my friends, will be *my* America.

INDEX

ABA. *See* American Basketball Association
Abdul-Aziz, Zaid, 94
Abdul-Jabbar, Kareem, 42–43, 45, 46–47, 93–94, 158–62, 207
Abdul-Rahman, Mahdi, 40, 94, 127
Abdul-Rauf, Mahmoud, 94, 206–7
Abernathy, Ralph, 197
ABL. *See* American Basketball League
Adams, Don, 128, 130, 139–42
Adderley, Herb, 13, 31–32
Adelman, Rick, 132
Africa, 113–14, 225–27
African Americans
    as athletes, 33
    civil rights movement to, 81–83
    coaching by, 68–69, 94–95, 132–35
    drugs and, 108
    equality for, 5
    goodwill among, 56
    HBCUs and, 18, 73, 96–98, 206, 210–12, 228
    in higher education, 17–18, 167–68, 208–9
    Islam to, 89–90, 93–94, 206–7
    Jewish people and, 20–23
    leadership of, 89–90
    in Los Angeles, 162
    Motown music to, 79
    NBA and, xiii, 19–20, 36, 39–40, 74–75, 95–101, 113–14, 206–10
    as NBA Coach of the Year, 3, 132–35
    New York City for, 57–58
    at Olympics, 40, 99
    in Philadelphia, 3
    police and, 225
    in politics, 193–94, 197
    poverty and, 82
    prejudice against, 34–35
    professionalism of, 76
    racial discrimination against, 13
    racial justice to, 83–87
    racism against, 17, 63–66
    respect to, 73
    St. Louis for, 59
    scouting of, 98–99
    segregation of, 18
    single mothers of, 9–10
    stereotypes of, 93–94
    in United States, 3–4, 90–91, 221–29
    Vietnam War to, 81–82
    in Washington DC, 10–11
    white people and, 13–14, 113–14, 187–88
    in World War II, 13
Agase, Alex, 172–75, 183
Alcindor, Lew, 93

alcohol abuse, 9–10
Alexander, Leroy, 29
Ali, Muhammad, xiv, 84–89, 169
Allentown Jets, 33–35
American Basketball Association (ABA), 70
    career in, 3, 55, 117–22
    NBA and, 30, 98–99, 120–21, 214–15
American Basketball League (ABL), 216
American Federation of Government Employees, 194
Al-Amin, Jamil Abdullah, 196–97
Ancheril, Phil, 187
Anderson, Jerry, 19
Andrews, Eddie, 201–2
Andrews, Hollis, 202
Andrews, Mark, 191–92, 201
Antetokounmpo, Giannis, 219
Anthony, Carmelo, 219
Anthony, Greg, 32
Archibald, Nate "Tiny," 148
Arizin, Paul, 21, 58, 98, 205
Armstrong, Jim, 26–27
athletes
    African Americans as, 33
    Auerbach with, 75
    charity by, 48
    college, 178–82
    competition with, 52
    free agency for, xiv
    from HBCUs, 210–12
    inspiration from, 11–12
    in NBA, 99–101, 171
    NBPA to, 61
    in NFL, 30, 206–7, 217
    psychology of, 42
    race of, 99–101
    uniform numbers to, 54–55
Attles, Al, 36, 44, 79–81, 133
Auerbach, Red, 20–24, 43, 75, 94, 97, 210, 213
BAA. *See* Basketball Association of America
Bacote, Ralph "The Durango Kid," 28
Baker, Charles, 29
Baker, Haley, 201
Baker League, xi, 28–30, 197
Baldwin, James, 53
Baltimore Bullets, xii, 103–12, 145–46
Barkley, Charles, 164, 208
Barksdale, Don, 209–10
Barnes, Jim, 40, 96
Barnett, Dick "Skull," 166
Barney, Lem, 184
Barnhill, John, 69–70, 106, 166
Barrett, Mike "Birdman," 118

Barry, Rick, 117–18, 121, 125
baseball, 55, 97, 217
basketball. *See also specific topics*
  in ABL, 216
  in Baker League, 28–30, 197
  cheap shots in, 53
  in EBL, 33–38, 50, 65, 106, 203, 211
  at EMU, 153, 167–69
  fouls in, 45–46
  higher education and, 166
  in high school, 12–15
  Jewish people in, 208
  at Kutsher's Country Club, 20–21
  at Madison Square Garden, 15, 58
  in NCAA, 157–58, 162, 169–73, 176–80
  in New York City, 196, 204
  at New York City Tech Junior College,
    18–19
  in Philadelphia, xi–xii, 58, 161, 205
  promotion of, 179–80
  race and, 224–29
  at Rucker Park, 28, 197
  at St. Francis, 95–96
  segregation in, 63–66
  State Department overseas tour, 79–81
  at UP, 25–28, 31–33
  at USF, 162
  at Western Community House, 10
  at West Philadelphia High School, 17
  in WNBA, 228–29
Basketball Association of America (BAA),
  19–20
Baylor, Elgin
  friendship with, 27
  inspiration from, 54, 211
  reputation of, 11–12, 36, 53
  in Seattle, 17, 27, 32
Beaty, Zelmo, 118, 215
Beck, Ernie, 205
Beckwith, Byron De La, 223
Bellamy, Walt
  inspiration from, 40, 60, 96, 165
  reputation of, 24, 38, 45, 47
Berbick, Trevor, 86
Bianchi, Al, 21, 118, 122, 124–25, 182
Biddy League, 10
Bill, Bill, 194
Billy Jack (film), 79
Bing, Dave "Bingo," 127
  Detroit Pistons and, 130–31, 139–43
  friendship with, 104, 142–43, 166
  reputation of, 69–70, 109, 123–25, 146–47
Bird, Larry, xiii, 157–64, 179, 213, 215–16
Bishop, Joey, 91
Black Lives Matter, 228
Black Panthers, 82–83, 93
Black people. *See* African Americans
Blake, Marty, 97, 210
Bockhorn, Arlen, 53

Boerwinkle, Tom, 132
Bonaparte, Maria, 88
Booker, Devin, 219
Boone, Pat, 117
Boone, Ron, 121
Boozer, Bob, 40
Born, B. H., 157
Borscht Belt, 20–22
Boston, 56, 161–63
Boston Celtics, 20–21, 110, 158–64. *See also specific*
  players
Boston Red Sox, 163
Bowman, Nate, 112
boxing, 57, 84–89, 169
Boyce, Jim, 178
Bradds, Gary, 117
Bradley, Bill, 30, 58, 110
Braun, Carl, 21
Brazil, 81
Brennan, Pete, 34
Brickley, James, 167, 174–75
Bridges, Bill, 79–81, 95
Brooke, Edward, 90
Brown, Charley, 17
Brown, Freddie "Downtown," 111, 142
Brown, Herb, 149–50
Brown, H. Rap, 196–97
Brown, Hubie, 34
Brown, Larry, 118, 149
Brown, Mike, 135
Brown, Roger, 153
Brown, Timmy, 30
Brown, Tony, 228
Bryant, Emmette, 112
Bryant, Hallie, 17
Bryant, Joe "Jellybean," 214
Bryant, Kobe, 214
Bryant, Ray, 56
Budd, Dave, 64
Buffalo Braves, 112–13
Burleson, Tom, 142
Burton, Al, 34
Butcher, Donnis, 69
Butler, Al, 20
Caldwell, Joe "Pogo," 40, 69, 98
Cambage, Liz, 228
Card, Frank, 117
Carrier, Darel, 98
Carter, George, 87, 98–99
Casey, Dwane, 135
Cassell, Mitchell, 201
Catholicism, 26
Chamberlain, Barbara, 48
Chamberlain, Selina, 48
Chamberlain, Wilt, xiii
  with athletes, 30
  career of, 157, 161, 205
  inspiration from, 41–43
  leadership of, 110, 211

at Overbrook High School, 13
Philadelphia to, 14
promotion of, 58
reputation of, 162
success of, 24, 44–48, 125–26
with teammates, 21–22
Chaney, Don, 134
Chaney, James, 224
Chaney, John, 29
charity, 48, 195–96
Chauvin, Derek, 225
cheap shots, 53
Cheeks, Mo, 30
Chenier, Phil, 146
Chicago, 56
Chicago Bulls, 164–65
childhood, 9–13
China, 81–82
Chisholm, Shirley, 90
Chuvalo, George, 88–89
Cincinnati, 56
civil rights movement, 79–83, 90–91, 222–24
Clark, Archie, 60, 127, 142, 146
Clark, Dean, 27
Clay, Cassius. *See* Ali
Clemens, Barry, 121
Clifton, Nathaniel "Sweetwater," 74, 209
coaching
    by African Americans, 68–69, 94–95, 132–35
    by Auerbach, 43
    with Detroit Pistons, 3, 123–32, 137–43, 147–53
    at EMU, 153, 169, 175–85, 188
    by Ferry, 145–46
    inspiration from, 122
    by McGuire, 67–68, 75, 77, 122
    NBA Coach of the Year, 3, 132–35
    with youth, 197–202
Cofield, Fred, 188
Cohen, Haskell, 19–22, 148–49, 210
Coil, Ed, 124, 126–28, 137–38, 141
college athletes, 178–82
Collins, Addie Mae, 223
Colonial Life & Accident, 189, 192–95
Como, Perry, 79
compensation, to college athletes, 178–80
competition, 52, 212–13
Connally, Doug, 122
Converse shoes, 163
Cook, Darwin, 32
Cooke, Jack Kent, 58, 60–61
Cooper, Chuck, 73, 208
Cooper, Michael, 160
Counts, Mel, 103
Cousy, Bob "Cooz," 20–21, 51, 97
Covington, Robert, 97
Cowens, Dave, 47, 161–62
Crawford, Freddie, 28
Crawford, Joey, 29
Cuban, Mark, 228

Cunningham, Billy "Kang," 43, 91, 97–98
Curry, Stephen, 164, 218
Dampier, Louie, 98
Dandridge, Bob, 111, 146, 153
Dangerfield, Rodney, 23, 119
D'Antoni, Mike, 216
Davidson, Bill, 138, 141, 147, 152
Davies, Bob, 95
Davis, Jim, 126
Dawkins, Darryl, 30, 100, 213–14
DeBusschere, Dave, 55, 68–70, 109–10, 166
Dele, Bison, 94
Detroit, 57, 99, 165, 169, 170. *See also specific topics*
Detroit Pistons
    career with, xi–xii, 67–70
    Chicago Bulls and, 164–65
    coaching with, 3, 123–32, 137–43, 147–53
    draft selection of, 37–38
    reputation of, 31–32
    rookie year with, 4, 37, 49–55, 68
    success with, 132–35
    trade from, 103–4
DeZonie, Hank, 208
Diamond, Neil, 129
Dickerson, Henry, 153
Dischinger, Terry, 109
discrimination, 4, 13, 100
Dončić, Luka, 219
Donne, Elena Delle, 228
Donovan, Eddie, 112
draft, NBA, 37–38, 69–70
Drexler, Clyde, 164
drugs, 9–10, 90, 108
Dukes, Walter, 14, 20, 212
Dundee, Angelo, 87
Duquesne University, 15, 19, 207–8
Dylan, Bob, 79, 219
Eakins, Jim "Jumbo," 118–19
early life, 9–15
Eastern Michigan University (EMU)
    basketball at, 153, 167–69
    coaching at, 153, 169, 175–85, 188
    recruitment at, 169–75
    social life at, 185–86
Eastern Professional Basketball League (EBL),
    33–38, 50, 65, 106, 203, 211
Easy Rider (film), 79
Eberhard, Al, 151
EBL. *See* Eastern Professional Basketball League
Ebony (magazine), 13, 222
Egan, Johnny "Space," 64, 105
Eisenhower, Dwight, 13–14
Ellington, Duke, 138
Elliott, Bob, 170, 182
Ellis, Leroy, 105
Embry, Wayne, 79–81
Empire of Ghana, 227
EMU. *See* Eastern Michigan University
Engelbert, Kurt, 106

Erving, Julius "Dr. J.," 120, 164, 165
Evans, Earnest, 91
Evers, Medgar, 223
Ewing, Patrick, 164
Fairmount Park, 11
fans, 204–5
A Farewell to Arms (film), 27
Farmer, Mike, 203–4
Farr, Mel, 184
Feldman, Oscar, 138, 147, 149, 151–52
Felix, Ray, 20, 36, 208–9
Fenton, Bob, 169, 173–74
Ferry, Bob, xii, 44, 81–83, 145–46, 147
Fitch, Bill, 134
Fitzsimmons, Cotton, 134, 148
Fleisher, Larry, 60
Floyd, George, 225, 228
Ford, Chris, 130–31, 151
Foreman, Earl, 107, 117–18, 120, 122
Foreman, George, 86, 88
fouls, in basketball, 45–46
the Four Tops, xii, 57
Franklin, Aretha, 57, 104–5
Frazier, Darnella, 225
Frazier, Joe, xiv, 85–86, 88
Frazier, Marvis, 86
Frazier, Walt "Clyde," 98, 109–11
Free, Lloyd B., 24
free agency, xiv, 104
Freund, Al, 167
friendship
    with Baylor, 27
    with Bing, 104, 142–43, 166
    with Chamberlain, W., 47–48
    with Lloyd, 73–78, 123–25, 142–43, 212–13
    with teammates, 19
Fulks, "Jumpin'" Joe, 97
Gaines, Clarence, 17–18, 63
Gaines, David "Smokey," 170, 178
Gaines, Dick, 14
Galento, Tony "Two Ton," 88
Gallatin, Harry "The Horse," 97
Garner, Bill "Slim," 32
Garnett, Kevin, 214
Garrett, Dick, 112
The Gillette Cavalcade of Sports (radio show), 88
Gilliam, Herm, 112
Gilmore, Artis, 215
Ginakes, Nick, 193–94
Gladys Knight & the Pips, xii
Gola, Tom, 205
Goodman, Andrew, 224
Goodrich, Gail, 125
Gordon, Russell, 29
Gottlieb, Eddie, 58–60
Gourdine, Simon, 140
Grange, Red, 46
Green, Carl, 47, 196
Green, Jerry, 150

Green, Johnny "Jumpin'," 17, 36, 45, 64, 105
Green, Sihugo, 15, 36, 208
Green, Victor Hugo, 11
Greer, Hal, 43
Grevey, Kevin, 111, 146
Griner, Brittney, 228
Guerin, Richie, 21, 24–25, 53, 64, 80–81
Hagan, Cliff, 27, 65
Hairston, Lindsay, 153
Haley, Alex, 53
Hall of Fame, 45
Harlem Globetrotters, 73–74
Harris, Ron, 88
Hart, Tom, 106
Haskins, Clem, 146
Havlicek, John, 96, 162, 166
Hawkins, Connie, 30
Hawkins, Robert "Bubbles," 171
Hayes, Elvin, 111, 145–46, 147
Haywood, Spencer, 99–100, 142
Hazzard, Walt, 40, 94, 112
HBCUs. *See* Historically Black Colleges and
    Universities
Heathcote, Jud, 173
Heinsohn, Tom, 20–21, 51, 208, 210–11
Hemingway, Ernest, 53–54
Hemphill, Tyrone, 129
Henderson, Fletcher, 208
Henderson, Tom, 146
Hennessy, Larry, 205
Hetzel, Fred, 121
Heyman, Artie, 24–25
higher education. *See also specific topics*
    African Americans in, 17–18, 167–68, 208–9
    basketball and, 166
    at HBCUs, 18, 73, 96–98, 206, 210–12, 228
    NCAA and, 157–58, 162, 169–73, 176, 180
    race in, 205–6
    recruitment at, 17–18
    segregation in, 14
high school, 12–17, 41, 213–14
Hightower, Wayne, 121
highways, 13–14
Hill, Cleo, 63–66
Hill, Sonny, 29, 33–35, 47–48, 106
Historically Black Colleges and Universities
    (HBCUs), 18, 73, 96–98, 206, 210–12, 228
Hoeft, Arnie, 60, 107
Hogue, Paul, 157
Holmes, Larry, 86
Holmes, Richard, 56
Holzman, Red, 35–36, 97, 110, 210
Hooks, Benjamin, 18
Hoover, Tom, 30
Hopkins, Bob, 209
Hornung, Paul, 31
Hosket, Bill, 112
Howard, John Samuel, 9
Howell, Bailey, 50–51, 53, 109

Hudgins, Gene, 34
Hudson, Rock, 27
Hughes, Langston, 53
Hummer, John, 112
Humphrey, Hubert, 90–91, 183–84
Hunter, Bobby "Zorro," 28
injuries, 24, 119–20, 151, 209
Inniss, Al, 14
inspiration
    from athletes, 11–12
    from Baylor, 54, 211
    from Bellamy, 40, 60, 96, 165
    from Chamberlain, W., 41–43
    in childhood, 15
    from coaching, 122
    from Ferry, 145–46
    from King, Martin Luther, Jr., 77–78, 127
    from Lloyd, 122, 133, 166, 182, 206
institutional racism, 178
Ionescu, Sabrina, 228
Iron Dukes, 207–8
Irvine, George, 118
Islam, 89–90, 93–94, 206–7
Jackson, Chris, 94, 206–7
Jackson, Jackie, 28
Jackson, Jesse, 90, 197
Jackson, Luke, 30, 40
Jacobs, Boston, 88–89
James, LeBron, 164, 213–14, 218–19
Japan, 81–82
Jefferson, Arthur, 194
Jet (magazine), 13, 222
Jeter, Eugene "Pooh," 32
Jeter, Hal, 117
Jewish people, 20–23, 208, 224
JFK. *See* Kennedy, John F.
Jim Crow laws, 11, 108, 221
John, Elton, 129
John Bartram High School, xi
Johnson, Andy, 26, 37, 80
Johnson, Avery, 134
Johnson, Charles, 146
Johnson, Dennis, 111
Johnson, Earvin "Magic," xiii, 157–64, 173, 182, 213, 215–16
Johnson, Gus, 105, 109, 121, 166
Johnson, John, 111
Johnson, Lyndon Baines, 39–40, 91
Johnson, Neil, 27, 87, 98, 118
Jokić, Nikola "The Joker," 219
Jones, Jennifer, 27
Jones, Jimmy, 146
Jones, K. C., 17, 51
Jones, Sam, 51
Jones, Willie, 36, 213
Jordan, Michael, 164–65, 215–16
Jordon, Phil, 64
Kaepernick, Colin, 206–7
Kaline, Al, 169

Kauffman, Bob, 112
Keller, Billy, 98
Kellogg, Junius, 15
Kelso, Ben, 130
Kennedy, John F. (JFK), 4–5, 39–40, 223–24
Kerner, Ben, 63
Kerr, Johnny, 52
Kerr, Steve, 228
Kimock, Johnny, 35
King, Coretta Scott, 91
King, Martin Luther, Jr.
    assassination of, 91, 108, 224
    leadership of, 77–78, 82, 84, 127, 196
King, Maurice, 39
Kingdom of Aksum, 227
Kingdom of Kush, 227
Kirkland, Courtney, 228
Knowings, Herman, 28
Kojis, Don, 80
Kupchak, Mitch, 146
Kutsher, Helen, 21
Kutsher, Milt, 21–23
Kutsher's Country Club, 20–25, 47
LaCour, Fred, 65
Lacy, Carl, 13
Laimbeer, Bill, 165
Land of Punt, 227
Lanier, Bob, 123–26, 130–31, 161
Lantz, Stu, 131, 139
Lapchick, Joe, 210
LaRusso, Rudy, 67–68, 103–4, 109, 166
Layton, Mo, 140
LCFS. *See* Lutheran Child and Family Services
Lear, Hal "King," 14, 29, 157
Lee, George, 51
Lee, Spike, 164, 216
Levane, Fuzzy, 35, 65
Lewis, Alvin "Blue," 88
Lewis, Hedgemon, 88
LIFE (magazine), 222
Ligon, Billy, 140
Ligon, Jim "Goose," 99
Lillard, Damian, 219
little people, 201–2
Little People's Tournament, 201–2
Liuzzo, Viola, 224
Lloyd, Earl, 68
    friendship with, 73–78, 123–25, 142–43, 212–13
    inspiration from, 122, 133, 166, 182, 206
    scouting by, 36–38, 49, 97, 210
Loeffler, Kelly, 229
Logan, Henry, 117
Lolich, Mickey, 169
Lombardi, Vince, 31
Los Angeles, 57, 162
Los Angeles Lakers, 158–64
Loscutoff, Jim, 203–4
Loughery, Kevin "Murph," 55, 105, 109, 148
Louis, Joe, 46, 84, 88

Love, Bob "Butterbean," 130, 132
Lovellette, Clyde, 65
Lower Merion High School, 214
Lucas, Jerry, 96, 157
Lumpp, Ray, 18
Lutheran Child and Family Services (LCFS), 195–196
Mackey, John Raymond, 9, 108
MacLeod, John, 140
Madison Square Garden, 15, 58
Mahorn, Ricky, 97, 165
Malcolm X, 53, 82, 84, 89–90, 127, 196, 224
Mali Empire, 227
Malone, Karl, 164
Malone, Moses, 163
Maloy, Mike, 87, 118
Maravich, "Pistol" Pete, 97, 139
March Madness, 180
marijuana, 90
Marin, Jack, 107, 109, 121, 145
marriage, 190
Martin, Pep, 35–36
Martin, Trayvon, 225
Mason, Anthony, 97
Maurie (film), 208
May, Don, 112
McCabe, Mick, 178
McCann, Brendan, 34, 106
McCann, Les, xii, 57, 107
McCracken, Branch, 17
McCullough, Bob, 28
McGinnis, George, 24
McGuire, Dickie, 37–38, 50–52, 67–68, 75, 77, 122, 182
McHale, Kevin, 158
McKinney, Horace "Bones," 64
McKinney, Jack, 160
McLendon, John, 166
McMillon, Shellie, 36, 65
McNair, Carol Denise, 223
media, 204–5
Mefford, Mary Lynn, 198
Meminger, Dean, 111
Mengelt, John, 128, 130, 151
Meschery, Tom, 67–68, 109, 166
Michigan State University, 158
Mikan, George, 46–47, 54, 73, 98
Miles, Eddie, 70, 104
Mingus, Charles, 107
Minor, Davage "Dave," 209
Mitchell, Sam, 135
Moe, Doug, 118, 149
Molinas, Jack, 211
Money, Eric, 139, 151, 171
Monroe, Earl "The Pearl," 81, 98, 108–9, 111, 158
Moore, Donald "Dudey," 19, 208
Motown music, 79
Motta, Dick, 147
Mount, Rick, 98, 121
Murdock, Donavon, 200

Murrey, Dorie, 69
Musial, Stan, 63
music, xii, 23, 56–57, 79, 104–5, 181, 186
Nápoles, José, 88
Nash, Bobby, 130, 139
National Basketball Association (NBA)
    ABA and, 30, 98–99, 120–21, 214–15
    Abdul-Jabbar in, 42–43
    African Americans and, xiii, 19–20, 36, 39–40, 74–75, 95–101, 113–14, 206–10
    athletes in, 99–101, 171
    BAA and, 19–20
    cities of, 56–59
    Coach of the Year, 3, 132–35
    competition in, 212–13
    draft, 37–38, 69–70
    expansion of, 59, 214–15
    Hall of Fame, 45
    HBCUs and, 206
    owners, 58, 60–61
    players union, xiv
    politics in, xii
    professionalism in, 54, 213–14
    promotion of, 163, 215–2116
    in Puerto Rico, 153
    racial discrimination in, 100
    racism in, 40–41, 65, 140, 224–25
    referees in, 29
    rivalries in, 157–64
    Robertson, O., and, 59–61, 101
    rookie year in, 4, 203–6, 210–11
    scouting by, 35–36, 96
    success of, 157–66
    with 3-pointers, 216–19
    trades in, 145–46, 160–61
    WNBA and, 228–29
    work ethic in, 27–28
National Basketball Players Association (NBPA), 61
National Collegiate Athletic Association (NCAA), 157–58, 162, 169–73, 176–80. *See also specific topics*
Naulls, Willie, 17, 50, 64
NBA. *See* National Basketball Association
NBPA. *See* National Basketball Players Association
NCAA. *See* National Collegiate Athletic Association
Negratti, Al, 25–28
The Negro Motorist Green Book (Green, V. H.), 11, 14
Nelson, Don, 60
Netolicky, Bob, 121
New York City
    for African Americans, 57–58
    basketball in, 196, 204
    culture in, 76
    New York City Tech Junior College, 18–19
    Philadelphia and, 30
    Rucker Park in, 28

New York Knicks, 20, 25, 109–11
New York University (NYU), 18
New York Yankees, 163
NFL, 30, 206–7, 217
Nike, 164, 215–16
Nixon, Norm, 160–61
Noble, Chuck, 67–68
Norman, Coniel "Popcorn," 171
Norman, Jay, 14, 29
Norwood, Willie, 133, 139
NYU. *See* New York University
Oakland Squires, 117
Oakley, Charles, 97
Ohl, Don, 51
Olajuwon, Hakeem, 164
Olympics, 40, 63, 93, 99, 201–2
O'Neal, Jermaine, 213–14
O'Neill, Shaquille, 47, 95, 218
O'Quinn, Kyle, 97
Oswald, Lee Harvey, 223
Outlaw's Son (film), 27
Overbrook High School, 13, 41
owners, in NBA, 58, 60–61
Page, Patti, 79
Palazzi, Togo, 208
Panel, Wally, 26
Parade (magazine), 19
Parham, Tee, 29
Parish, Robert, 54, 158
Parker, Candace, 228
Patterson, Floyd, 84–85, 88
Paulson, Jerry, 106
Paultz, Billy "The Whopper," 215
Payne, Freda, 57
Pep, Willie, 89
Pettit, Bob "Big Blue," 53, 65, 97
Philadelphia
    African Americans in, 3
    Baker League in, 28–30
    basketball in, xi–xii, 58, 161, 205
    to Chamberlain, W., 14
    childhood in, 9
    Fairmount Park in, 11
    Lower Merion High School, 214
    New York City and, 30
    South Catholic High School, 12–13
    Washington DC compared to, 4
    West Philadelphia High School, 13, 17, 41
Philadelphia Warriors, 26, 36, 44, 59
Philippines, 81–82
Phillis Wheatley Recreation Center, 10
Pitts, Elijah, 31
police, 225, 228
politics, xii, 90–91, 193–94, 196, 197
Pollin, Abe, 107
Popovich, Gregg, 228
Porter, Howard, 141–42, 148
Porter, Kevin, 146, 148–51
poverty, 10, 81–82

Powell, Boog, 108
Powell, Cincy, 32, 98–99
Powell, Clayton, 90
prejudice, xiii, 34–35, 93–94, 96
professionalism, 54, 76, 213–14
promotion, 58, 163, 179–80, 215–2116
psychology, 10–11, 42
Puerto Rico, 61, 153
Quarry, Jerry, 86
race
    of athletes, 99–101
    Baltimore Bullets and, 107–8
    basketball and, 224–29
    in childhood, 12–13
    in higher education, 205–6
    poverty and, 81
    prejudice and, xiii
    in United States, xiv
racial bias, 12
racial discrimination, 4, 13, 100
racial inequality, 4–5
racial justice, 83–87, 221–29
racism
    against African Americans, 17, 63–66
    to Auerbach, 23
    in Boston, 56, 161
    institutional, 178
    in NBA, 40–41, 65, 140, 224–25
    outside United States, 79–81
    by referees, 175–76
    strategies for, 107
    in United States, 188–89, 191
    violence and, 221–26, 228
radio career, 169, 191–92
Ramsey, Cal, 39
Ramsey, Frank, 51
Rand, Ayn, 107
Rauch, Mike, 198
Ray, Clifford, 132
reading, 53–54
recruitment, 17–19, 25–26, 35–36, 169–75
Reed, Willis, xiii, 47, 82–83, 110–11, 161, 166
referees, 29, 175–76, 228
religion, 26
Ricketts, Dick, 207
Riddle, Bob, 175
Riegle, Don, 183–84
Riley, Pat, 160
Riordan, Mike, 146
rivalries, in NBA, 157–64
Rivers, Doc, 134, 228
Robertson, Carole Rosamond, 223
Robertson, Oscar
    leadership of, xiv, 40
    NBA and, 59–61, 101
    reputation of, 109, 197, 211, 219
Robinson, Brooks, 108
Robinson, David, 164
Robinson, Flynn, 125–26

Robinson, Frank, 108
Robinson, Jackie, 14, 46
Robinson, Leonard "Truck," 97, 146
Robinson, Sugar Ray, 84, 88
Rodgers, Guy, 14, 29, 96, 101, 148, 205
Rodman, Dennis, 54, 165
Rondo, Rajon, 219
rookie year, 4, 37, 49–55, 68, 203–6, 210–11
Rosenbluth, Lennie, 162
Rowe, Curtis, 123, 128, 130, 139–42, 151
Rowland, Dennis, 129
Rucker Park, 28, 197
Rudolph, Mendy, 21
Russell, Bill, xiii, 51
　Chamberlain, W., and, 43–44, 211
　injuries of, 21
　personality of, 165–66
　as player-coach, 94–95, 133, 209
　reputation of, 46–47, 63, 157, 162
　in San Francisco, 17
Russell, Cazzie, 58, 69, 96, 125
Russell, John "Honey," 19
Russell, Walker D., 170, 182
Ruth, Babe, 46
St. Francis, 14–15, 95–96
St. Louis, 59, 63–65
Sam, Al, 186
Sample, Johnny "Red Ball," 30
Sanders, Charlie, 184
Sanders, Tom "Satch," 36, 51, 110, 121
San Francisco, 17
San Francisco Warriors, 36, 44, 104
Saperstein, Abe, 216
Sauldsberry, Woody, 36
Schaus, Fred, 134
Schayes, Adolph "Dolly," 97, 210–11
Schayes, Dolph, 53, 74
Scheer, Carl, 112–13
Schockro, Doc, 127
scholarships, 18–19
Schulman, Sam, 100
Schulz, Laurie, 198
Schwerner, Michael, 224
Scott, Allison (daughter), 198–200
Scott, Byron, 135, 160–61
Scott, Charlie (no relation), 30, 99, 118–20, 215
Scott, David (son), 190
Scott, Debra (daughter), 190
Scott, Devon Marie (daughter), 200
Scott, John (son), 190
Scott, Karen (daughter), 190
Scott, Marvin (brother), 10–11, 194–95
Scott, Marvin, Jr. (nephew), 194–95
Scott, Nia (daughter), 200–201
Scott, Nicole (niece), 194–95
Scott, Roy. See specific topics
Scott, Sylvester Bernard (stepfather), 9, 87–88
Scott, Walter, 225
scouting, 35–36, 96, 98–99, 210

Seattle, 17, 27, 32
Seattle Supersonics, 100, 111, 146
segregation, 11, 14, 18, 23, 63–66
self-education, 53–54
service, 195–96
Seton Hall, 14–15, 19, 22, 26, 205
Seymour, Paul, 65
Sharman, Bill, 20–21
Shaw, Robert, 227
Shelton, Lonnie, 111
Shue, Gene, 51, 106, 112, 122, 124–25, 182
Siegfried, Larry, 38
Sikma, Jack, 111
Silas, Paul, 60, 95, 111
Silliman, Mike, 99, 112
Silver, Adam, 228
Simmons, Eddie "The Czar," 28
Simon, Walt, 28
Sims, Bobby, 65, 167
single mothers, 9–10
Slaughter, Jose, 32
Sloan, Jerry, 131–32
Smith, Don, 94
Smith, Elmore, 153
Smith, Eugene, 167, 171–73
Smith, Kate, 129
Smith, Odie, 80
Smith, Randy, 148
Sonhai Empire, 227
Soul Train (TV show), 129
South Catholic High School, 12–13
Spivey, Bill, 211
Spoelstra, Art, 34, 106
Spoelstra, Erik, 32
State Department overseas tour, 79–81
stereotypes, 93–94, 96
Stern, David, 215–16
Stith, Tom, 38
Stokes, Maurice, 15, 24, 95–96, 101, 208–10
Stokes, Vernon, 14
Strawder, Joe, 70
Strayhorn, Billy, 138
Supreme Court, 4–5
Swain, Ben, 209
"Sweet Caroline" (Diamond), 129
Syracuse, 59
Tarkanian, Jerry, 175
Taurasi, Diana, 228
Taylor, Jim, 31
Taylor, Roland "Fatty," 86–87, 118–19
teammates
　on Baltimore Bullets, xii, 105–6
　Chamberlain, W., with, 21–22
　friendship with, 19
　injuries of, 24
　lessons learned with, 50
　in rookie year, 68
the Temptations, xii, 57
Terrell, Ernie, 84–85

Thorn, Rod, 69, 148
3-pointers, 216–19
Thurmond, Nate, 47, 125
Tiebout, Bernie, 19
Till, Emmett, 221–23
Tormohlen, Gene, 80, 148
Torrance, Walter, 17
trades, 103–4, 145–46, 160–61
Trapp, George "Instant Heat," 128, 130–31
travel, 10–11
Tresvant, John, 69–70
Tucker, Jim, 74, 76, 208
Turman, Doc, 34
Turman, Roman, 211
Twyman, Jack, 23–24
Tyner, Herb, 152–53
uniform numbers, 54–55
Unitas, Johnny, 108
United States. *See also specific places*
   Africa compared to, 113–14
   African Americans in, 3–4, 90–91, 221–29
   Borscht Belt in, 20–22
   civil rights movement in, 79–83, 90–91,
      222–24
   culture in, xii, 56–59
   highways in, 13–14
   history of, xiii
   Jewish people in, 224
   JFK and, 39–40
   Jim Crow laws in, 11, 108, 221
   race in, xiv
   racial inequality in, 4–5
   racism in, 188–89, 191
   racism outside, 79–81
   segregation in, 11
   Supreme Court, 4–5
   travel in, 10–11
   white people in, 35
   working class in, 35
   in World War II, 13
University of Detroit, 99, 170
University of Kansas, 21–22, 41, 162
University of Nevada at Las Vegas (UNLV),
   175–76
University of Portland (UP), 25–28, 31–33
University of San Francisco (USF), 162
University of Seattle, 27
UNLV. *See* University of Nevada at Las Vegas
Unseld, Wes, 109, 111, 145–46
UP. *See* University of Portland
Uruguay, 80
USF. *See* University of San Francisco
Van Arsdale, Tom, 70
Van Lier, Norm, 131–32, 147
Vaughn, Chico, 69
Vietnam War, xii, 81–82, 91, 196
violence, 221–26, 228
Virginia Squires, 117–20, 122, 215
Walker, Chet "The Jet," 30, 43, 91, 98, 130, 132

Walker, Horace, 17
Wallace, Ben, 94, 97
Walton, Bill, 164
Wanzer, Bobby, 95
Warren, Rick, 117
Washington, Kermit, 111
Washington, Tom, 228
Washington DC, 4, 10–12
Watts, Donald "Slick," 111, 142
Weatherspoon, Nick, 146
Weiss, Bob, 131–32
Wesley, Cynthia Dionne, 223
West, Jerry "Zeke from Cabin Creek," 97, 109,
   125, 157
Western Community House, 10
Westphal, Paul, 162
West Philadelphia High School, 13, 17, 41
Wheatley, Phillis, 10
White, Hubie, 13, 30
White, Jo Jo, 99, 162
White, Sherman, 211
White, Ted, 105
white people, 11, 13–14, 35, 113–14, 187–88
white supremacy, 222–26
Wilkens, Lenny, 15, 65, 133–34, 209, 211
Wilkes, Keith "Jamaal," 94, 158
Wilkins, Dominique, 164
Williams, Art, 162
Williams, Brian, 94
Williams, Lou, 213–14
Williams, Monty, 135
Willoughby, Bill "Poodle," 213
Wilson, A'ja, 228
Wilson, George, 40
Winograd, Mickey, 208
Winters, Brian, 153
The Wire (TV show), 108
WNBA, 228–29
Wolf, Charles, 68
Wonder, Stevie, xii
Wood, Willie, 91
Woodstock festival, 79
work ethic, 27–28, 41–42
working class, 35
World War II, 13
Worthy, "Big Game" James, 158
Wright, Larry, 146
Wright, Richard, 53
Yardley, George, 27
Young, Andrew, 197
Young, Trae, 219
Youngman, Henry, 23, 119
   Ziehm, Debby, 187
Ziehm, Duane, 187
Ziehm, Jeannine, 187
Ziehm, Jennifer, 184–91, 193–95
Zimmerman, George, 225–26
Zollner, Fred, 38, 75, 124, 126–27, 137–38

Philly native JOHN RAYMOND "RAY" SCOTT's college career began at the University of Portland, and he was chosen as the fourth pick in the 1961 NBA draft by the Detroit Pistons. He spent six years with the Pistons, as a stand-out rebounder and deadly shooter from the perimeter, and another five years playing for other teams. Then in October 1972, Scott was promoted from assistant to head coach of the Detroit Pistons, thanks in part to the strong support from retiring coach Earl Lloyd who, a decade earlier, had scouted Scott and recommended that he be the Pistons top pick. Two years later he was named NBA Coach of the Year, the first African American to win the coveted award. From 1976 to 1979, Scott was men's basketball head coach at Eastern Michigan University. Today, Ray lives with his family in Eastern Michigan, not far from Detroit. This is his first book.

CHARLEY ROSEN is one of the most respected writers of books on basketball, including both fiction like *New York Times* Notable Book *The House of Moses All-Stars*, and nonfiction like his telling of the Jack Molinas story in *The Wizard of Odds*. He has also been a sports commentator, at FOXSports.com and HoopsHype.com. He lives in Woodstock, New York.

EARL "THE PEARL" MONROE played for fourteen years in the NBA with the Baltimore Bullets and New York Knicks. In 1990, he was inducted into the Naismith Memorial Basketball Hall of Fame.

Basketball in Catskills Rises to New Heights

Tall Athletes Work Out on Court After Work on Dishes

By WILLIAM R. CONKLIN
Special to The New York Times.

MONTICELLO, N. Y., Aug. 10 —Those who get closest to the tops of the Catskill Mountains here without climbing are eight altitudinous basketball players with a work-and-play summer

Clinic in Mountains Helps Put Players on Winning Road

Ray Scott Set To Join Pistons

Bob and John Ivory

Congratulate

Ray Scott

Head Coach of the rapidly improving Detroit Pistons

Pressure

Scott expects top Pistons to produce

their fans

227   RAY SCOTT   FWD/CT

A native of Philadelphia where he played high school ball against Wilt Chamberlain, Ray scored close to 11,000 points in 9 seasons in the NBA. One of the better playmaking big men in pro basketball, he was Pistons' team captain.

CAREER PRO STATISTICS

Bullets Face Pistons

By CHARLES McGEEHAN

Detroit Piston coach Ray Scott, who needs no introduction here, knows what it takes to win games. His success as Earl Lloyd's successor should have been the snub of Lloyd, you were only wh

—News Photo